5 STORIES
DOWN

5 STORIES DOWN

Sometimes you must fall to rise

CODY RIDENOUR

I dedicate this book to the many people that helped me to get to this point. Especially my immediate, and extended family. Not to mention Livia's family and Flutie. There are multitudes of people to thank for helping me get to where I am today. Some that I know, and many that I don't. A lot that I am still in contact with, and sadly some I am not. Regardless, I'm eternally grateful for each one of you what you did for me, especially my mom and Mitch.

Table of Contents

It all started with one single tear as the prayers continued. I opened my eyes, and the first thing I recognized was Uncle Billy and his family praying for me. Where was I? This slowly became the first time I understood the gravity of the situation. It was the initial moment I consciously realized something had happened, without knowing how dire the situation was and would be from this point on. The thing I didn't understand was how demanding and challenging this conscious effort was going to be as I was very slowly breaking through the coma.

Where it All
Began

I was unsure how to start this story, but I guess I should begin as far back as I can remember. That would make sense.

I started my life with my mother, Bridget Hyatt, and the person who contributed some of his genes, John Ridenour, and that was about it throughout his life. My biological father wasn't much of a father but I forgive him and hold no grudge. I was born on June 29th, 1991, in Baltimore, Maryland, named Cody William Ridenour. In the late '80s, John inherited a large fortune from his father, so he never really needed good skills or anything that would make a good businessman, but he tried regardless. My parents tell me he failed at least one year of high school. I figured that since his dad was so rich, he thought he didn't have to try at anything.

I don't have many memories of him, but I will never forget that I thought he was very unattractive, and I was always afraid to end up like him—overweight and unattractive. I will never understand what my mom saw in him. She always says she was the sacrificial lamb so my older brother, Brady, and I could be born. My mom is an incredibly beautiful woman. We indeed got our good looks from her. So, thanks, mom. I have a picture with her and me from when I was a baby, and she looks like a freaking supermodel! I'll look for it.

When John's father passed away, John inherited his father's very successful lumber company, and he ran it right into the ground. Eventually, they divorced. Here's my mother, divorced and living with her father and two sons. Did I mention I have an older brother who is my best friend and has been with me through everything? His name is Brady Ridenour. He is a year and a half older than me.

I don't have a lot of memories from my early childhood. I had a normal childhood until I was around five when my parents divorced. Upon the divorce, John remarried to an unpleasant woman, my unbalanced stepmother Hannah. She was not very nice to me, and I blocked out many of those memories. For anonymity purposes, I will change some real names. Since I'm currently watching the series Dark on Netflix with my typist, we were inspired to change some names in this story to ones in this show. It's a very fantastic show; you should watch it. I'm going to call my biological father, John, his real name. Sadly, he passed away, and my stepmother Hannah and my two stepsisters will be called the older Franziska and the younger Elisabeth.

The first thing I can say to you is that John never made me feel loved, and it all started when I was just a baby. He refused to ever hold me or didn't like to because I was born with red hair, even though I was a cute baby. He did not want a freckled, red-haired child, a ginger child. The joke is on him because I don't have freckles on my face, just elbows, shoulders, and knees. That's why I have always been so close with my mom. That should give you a little taste of the kind of person he was.

While my mom was living with her dad, John got married again to a woman with two daughters from her previous marriage and they were much older than us. I guess since John didn't love me a ton anyway, my abusive stepmom Hannah had free rein to treat me and Brady however she chose. I got it worse than Brady. It made sense; John liked Brady much more than me. Brady has dirty blond hair. Don't feel too bad for me; she also treated Brady poorly. You may be asking yourself, "Where was John during this abuse?" Well, he could not have cared less. We will get there.

Brady and I were very sheltered children while living with Hannah. We were locked in the basement all day, every day, until John got home from work. We were never allowed to do anything upstairs unless we went to the bathroom, ate lunch, or had our afternoon snack—a small box of raisins. We would get our revenge by peeing bchind the couch whenever we needed to go. They totally deserved it. The worst part of this was that we had no idea that this was not the way others were raised—not being allowed to leave the basement and not being allowed to have any friends either. How were we to know we were just little "dibbies" (kids). This trauma I experienced with Brady never really affected me until much later in my life. It was not until I started getting close to the end of this story that I ever explored this traumatic time.

Also, I have no idea why, but we were never allowed to play sports or do anything active. I feel it has to do with the fact that she was annoyed with taking care of us. We were not allowed to do much else except hang out in the basement, where there was no TV. "So, what did you do all day in the basement?" Well, I don't remember much, but Brady tells me we would play with matchbox cars and pee behind the couch. At the end of our time there, I remember that Brady and I played this game where Brady would look at me and say:
— Hey Cody, sniff my butt.
— Why? You`re going to fart in my face.
— No, I promise you, I won`t.
— Okay.
Reluctantly, I would agree, and lo and behold, Brady would fart in my face. We thought this was the funniest game. Bored, sheltered little children, don't judge us. It was funny at the time.

There was also one of those old 1990s computers

with those amusing and low-tech computer games that every computer came with, and they were entertaining to us. The basement was finished, with carpet, white walls, and no windows. There was only one piece of furniture: the peeing couch. On the far wall were a computer and a desk with a chair. There was not a ton of space to do activities, so that's why we played "Sniff My Butt," and we always smashed our matchbox cars together on a white box. On the big white box next to the couch.

While we were locked in the basement, John was busy destroying his current business, which he would soon bankrupt. He would permanently destroy the business by spending much more than he would make.

Again, Hannah had to give us permission to go upstairs to get any food or snacks. Brady and I got very good at sneaking around; Brady was much better than me at this and far braver. I was always scared of her. This happened multiple times in our childhood, where every single time we did something wrong or something that Hannah didn't like. For example, if we didn't finish the chores well enough, if we got in trouble at the house or school, or if we didn't finish the dinner she made because we didn't like the food or flavor. We would be sent to our room for the night at 7:30 p.m. with just a cheese sandwich. It was not great; the sandwich was a small dinner roll and one Kraft single. The roll was so small, and the cheese would fall off the bread. My bedtime was 7:30 the whole time that I lived with them. It sometimes sucked in the summer; all the kids were still outside playing in the neighborhood, and I could hear them, but I was already in bed. I guess because he was a year and a half older than me, he was allowed to stay up until 8. Now that I'm older, I know that when you are a child, your brain needs more sleep to grow. I guess there were some benefits and drawbacks, as you will see. She taught me a couple of good things throughout the years, like not being afraid to try different foods, how to clean well, and some discipline.

When I would go visit my mom at our Pop-Pop's house every other weekend, I got sick almost every night, throwing up because my body was so used to shutting down at 7:30 p.m. I couldn't eat past this time without vomiting, and this continued at least until middle school. My mom remembers that Hannah was very mean to me regarding my potty training. As I was learning to use the toilet, she would scold me for having any skid marks in my underwear. It was such a problem that my mom always put me in new clothes before I returned to Hannah. I was always so scared to poop around her that I would hold my poop until I had awful stomach aches or cramps until I finally had no choice. All because I would get yelled at for having marks on my underwear. I think the most conniving part of her was her treatment of my actual mom. She always told me to throw things at her when she would come to pick us up, usually my bottle, and she would ask me to call her, my mother, a b**** (female dog), not knowing what it meant because I was just a little kid or "dibby". I would do stuff like that on the weekends with her because I was afraid of going against her. I could write a lot about how abusive Hannah was, but I'll just give you some highlights of things we can remember. I blocked most of it out and am still trying to regain the memories. She would only let us watch a few movies, and they included "Charlie and the Chocolate Factory," "The Never-Ending Story," and "Fantasia," and we were not allowed to watch anything else on TV. My stepsisters were always allowed to watch whatever they wanted. Granted, these are some good flicks, but they get old watching over and over. I remember going to the Mormon church with her and Brady every Sunday, and John never had to go. Brady and I had to dress up for church every Sunday. I did not love it, and I'm sure that Brady felt the same, but I did enjoy the social aspect because it was a chance for us to meet other kids. I have faint memories of Hannah reading the Mormon Bible to me before bed some nights and the stories were surprising.

It was exactly like the South Park episode about the new Mormon student. South Park, Season 7, Episode 12. I'm not sure if it was a Mormon thing or just because she wanted to control us completely, but we were not allowed to have any friends either, only some kids at school, and we never once had a friend come over to our house. Also, I don't fully understand why she made us wear collared shirts and very tight pants every day for school — not very cool or comfortable.

The worst thing she did to me that I entirely clearly remember was one day when I was sick. Brady and I were eating breakfast on the glass dinner table with marble counters and an island (I'm sure it was expensive), and she made me some oatmeal, which I love. Since I was sick, I could not eat it, so she gave me some pink liquid medicine, and it was good. I remember taking the medication, and it tasted good, like bubble gum. I tried to continue eating my oatmeal but quickly puked in it. I have no idea why; maybe we were out of medicine. She made me eat the entire bowl that I had just thrown up in. I agreed. I was too afraid of her to say no, and I thought she would do the best for me, like any mother. Brady was watching as we had just gotten yelled at during this time. Brady remained chill while I was eating the oatmeal I had just thrown up.

Another thing she did that was a little gross was that she would mix the last of the milk with water to make it last a little bit longer to save money or something; we always called it dirty sock milk because it tasted like a dirty sock, or at least what we thought a dirty sock might taste like. Both of my stepsisters would drink the milk too. We laughed when we started calling it that since we were all drinking it.

Most holidays were normal for us, but the worst was always Halloween. It was somewhat annoying because Hannah would never let us wear masks with our costumes because, for some reason, she thought we could suffocate from wearing masks. I guess it's possible, but for some reason, she thought it was a genuine concern. So, we had to get our faces painted by her. She was not a terrible artist, but it was kind of dumb when everyone else wore masks. She would also always go into our candy to make sure there were no drugs, weapons, or things like that, although there never were, being in such a wealthy neighborhood. Then, she would use that excuse to take all the best candies for herself. I know, not cool.

The most trouble I had when living with them was maybe in third grade. Hannah was checking my school folder to see my homework for the night, but to her surprise, she found something she had not expected. My best friend, Vinnie, and I thought it would be funny to write down as many cuss words as possible inside my folder. It's been so long now that I have no idea how many cuss words were on there, but it couldn't have been many. We were in elementary school. It was enough for me to get a cheese sandwich for dinner, my mouth washed out with soap, and some spankings on my buttocks, justified.

Another thing that I never understood until I got older was that Brady and I had the job of cleaning the bathrooms and toilets in the house. We didn't realize until later that it was because it was a crappy job, pun intended, that no one else wanted to do. Not just the bathrooms but the toilets. Our stepsisters had some chores also, though when they didn't complete the chores, we had to finish theirs.

Franziska is older than Elisabeth, but both were older than Brady and me. They were both tall and pretty. Franziska was an older, much meaner version of Elisabeth when we lived together. I cannot recall a single negative recollection of Elisabeth; she was consistently pleasant, amusing, and cool. Franziska had a lot more of Hannah's personality. She was a lot like the stepsisters in Cinderella. Franziska did what she wanted to do regardless of anyone else's feelings. I always thought Elisabeth must have had more of her dad's personality because she was just great.

Next, let's go to what Hannah looked like. Well, I always thought she was attractive. She had very dark brown hair that was not very long. She was averagely tall for a woman and was not dark by any means. She was pretty pale, had dark brown eyes, and was fit, I remember she was very into the amount of money that John had. She had relatively short hair and was average height for a girl—maybe a little short, but her daughters were tall.

Once a in a while, we would all go out to dinner as a family. We would either go to these restaurants called Bare Bones, a rib place, or this awesome Mexican place called Don Pablo's! Which was always my favorite; I always enjoyed those dinners.

Now that I think about it, taking a tour of the house we lived in, I'm unsure if I ever saw the stepsisters' room, or at least I don't remember seeing it. Hannah always said it was a mini-mansion; they were always, and they were both very proud of that fact. They had a room or rooms upstairs. I don't think I ever saw the master bedroom, either. The first thing you see when entering the house is a large chandelier. John always had to show off his money. The next thing you would see was the stairs to the second floor, where the bedrooms were. The first room you would walk past was John's office, but I would never go there. Right next to that room were the kitchen and then the dining table, next to each other. Next was the family room next to the kitchen, where you could see the basement door, which was Brady and me's daytime space. Right next to the food closet, at the end of the tour, was a large family room with a huge television. We would sometimes watch movies on laser discs and things like that. The dinner table was big and glass with nice chairs. I think the counters were marble, and they included an island. I can't remember what the sofas looked like or what they were made from, but we didn't spend too much time upstairs. I'll do what I can to remember the details, but it's been long. As for Franziska and Elisabeth, they were both a lot older than Brady and me. Franziska was around 13 or 14, and Elisabeth was the younger one, probably one or two years younger.

I remember that when Hannah cleaned, she would always listen to classical music; it was always classical. Which I thought was very boring, but to each their own.

A great thing about my mom is that she always listened to awesome music. There was also a nice pool and pool house behind the house. Anyone who has ever been to Maryland will know that the state is very hilly. Our house was on a massive hill with a large, winding driveway. It was great for sledding when it snowed. Now that I think about it, I don't have any memories of playing in the snow with John, my stepsisters, or my stepmom just Brady. Hannah put so much fear in us that one day, we were outside playing in the snow, and my mom just happened to be near their house and decided to stop to see her kids. When she did, instead of us showing excitement, all we could offer was fear of punishment if Hannah saw us talking to our mother. Something similar happened one Christmas; my mom was at a store returning a gift, and my mom just happened to be at the same store we were at with Hannah. We had to hide under a hanging coat rack. I think the dastardliest thing this woman did was change all our school papers, showing that she was our mom, deleting our true mother from our lives completely.

There was one time I can remember faintly when one of our sisters came to show her friend the house tour, including the basement. During the tour, I remember one of the sisters complaining about the smell near the couch. I thought it was funny because I knew what the smell was. She said it smelled like pee.

This is off-topic, but the other day, my mom explained that my hairline was starting to look slightly like John's, which upset me. It makes sense that my hairline is doing things, being 31 at this point, but I was hoping I would never get any of his genetics. Sadly, as we all know that's just not how genetics work. It upset me because he never felt like family to me, and he was a troubled man in his life. He is the definition of a sociopath and a narcissist. For the readers who don't know, these are the definitions of each. "Sociopath is a noun; a person with a personality disorder, manifesting itself in extreme anti-social attitudes and behaviors and a lack of conscience." "A narcissist is also a noun: a person with one of several personality disorders in which people have an inflated sense of their importance, a deep need for extensive attention and admiration, and troubled relationships." Sadly, this 100% describes John to a "T," which is precisely why he has no idea what happened when he was not at home. I'm sure nothing would have changed much had he known.

I feel bad for John, and I forgive him and Hannah. His whole life, he has never cared about anything except his money and showing it off. Money he never made himself. He never worked for it; he got it from his parents or stole it from his family. If you don't dislike him yet, that's about to change. This might be the worst thing he ever did, even worse than ditching his kids. His mother, my grandma, was fighting Alzheimer's, a severe case. He took this as an opportunity to change her will and take us completely out, to give himself more. There's more to this particular part of the awfulness that was John. We will get there later. Luckily for Brady and myself, my mom married the most incredible man I have ever met. A man named Mitchell Hyatt. A man that both Brady and I consider our dad! Before my mom ever met Mitch, she worked three jobs to support Brady, me, and herself. She did what she had to do. She's incredibly strong, as you will see as the story progresses.

The first time I fell in love with Mitch was when I still lived with John, and he signed me up for a basketball team. He was one of the coaches because I had to miss every other game when I was with John. Mitch invited him to every game I played, but he never came. I fell in love with basketball because of Mitch. For the rest of my life, I always loved the sport.

It's unbelievable, but Mitch and my mom went to high school together with John. They didn't know each other, even though they had many of the same friends. Given that John's parents spoiled him, he never had to work and didn't care. I'm pretty sure he never graduated, either. A few years after high school, Mitchell, and my mom worked for two companies, and both were invited to the same charity dance. Since neither my mom nor Mitch had a date to the dance, one of the bosses said they should go together. Before they could go to the dance, my mom wanted to meet Mitch at a bar to see if they were a good match and have an excellent time there. They had a great time at the bar and decided to go to the dance together. Mitch had such a great time at the dance that he got home and told his roommate that he was going to marry that girl! They've been married ever since. Mitch was not looking for a wife then, especially one with two sons already. Thank God my mom made a great first impression and married that man. He made me the man I am now with the help of my mom, family, Brady, and a few friends. It all started with Brady and me living with Mitch and my mom. I feel like that's really where my real life began. I'm sure that Brady would say the same. We were no longer confined only to the basement.

Real Life

Start

First, this is how my mom and Mitch got into the very long and expensive trial that got Brady and me out of that living situation with John and how my mom and Mitch took over our livelihoods. Thank God. I'm unsure where our lives would have gone without Mitch and Mom.

Since I was not around for this part of the story, I had Mitch and my mom talk me through the expensive and frustrating process of how they got custody of Brady and myself. Initially, my mom and Mitch only had us every other weekend. John and Hannah had us all during the week. By this point, my mom and Mitch had their first son, Devin Hyatt, in March, 1996. Every other weekend, Devin was always so excited to see us. We were both very happy to see him too. Then, out of nowhere, John decided to move to North Carolina with Brady and me without telling my mom or Mitch. Mitch's neighbor was his lawyer at the time, so when John called Mitch to tell him, not my mom, that he was leaving and moving to North Carolina, Mitch went right over to his place, and the next day he got an emergency junction to keep the kids in Maryland. Regardless, John still moved to North Carolina that weekend. I can only speculate on the kind of crazy emotions my mom was feeling when she got the news that John was taking Brady and me to another state. My guess is that they were not great. John had the movers already working on his move. He thought his moving would keep him out of the injunction process, but it did not thankfully. He was not allowed to leave the state of Maryland until the trial started because of the injunction. During that time, Brady and I lived with our grandmother Caroline, John's mom, whom we loved dearly. I am unsure how long we lived with her, but it was probably around a year or two during the trial. It was a long process, but it had to be so we could live in the correct place. I don't remember this; it was a long time ago. Brady and I shared a lawyer, a doctor, and a therapist for the entire spiel.

John and his wife, that crazy lady, decided to create a fake journal to make my mom look like a lunatic. They tried to create the illusion that my mother was not fit to raise children when they were the ones not fit to raise us. As the process progressed, Hannah and John lied through their teeth about everything they could to take custody from my mom. It was crazy, but their whole plan was to eventually delete my mom from our lives completely. Hannah even put her name as our mom on all school papers for no reason but to hurt my mom because my mom loved us, to make life more difficult for her.

Grandma Caroline, John's mom, had a new husband named Jim after her first husband, John's dad, died. This man, named Jim, smoked more cigarettes than any man I have ever met to this point in my life, and I highly doubt that will ever change. The only thing I remember him doing was watching golf and giving Brady and me the job of cutting his cigarette boxes for coupons. He was kind of just your classic grumpy old man who smoked a ton of cigarettes. Mitch told me he talked to him several times, and they shared their dislike of John. It was curious, but Jim had the same dislike of John that they all did, and he would talk to Mitch about it. Throughout the whole trial, John and Hannah did their best to lie and make my mom sound like a monster when I had been living with the real monster for years. They lied through their teeth the entire trial to make my mom sound terrible and make them look like angels. Thankfully, the judge was not buying any of it. Mitch is Jewish, so John and Hannah told the judge that Mitch never let us celebrate Christmas. It was obvious that they were lying once Mitch showed home video footage from past Christmases. When the judge at the custody hearing saw all the home videos from our Christmas together, the judge had had enough of the liars' tales. Another crazy thing that Hannah was doing throughout the whole trial process was continually telling me and Brady that my mom was not pregnant. She was obviously pregnant with our second half-brother, Shane Hyatt, who was born in June, 2000, the first day of summer. I still don't understand the point of saying or lying about that, but that was her choice. When Mitch got the email or letter from John's lawyer that he was leaving for North Carolina and taking Brady and me with him, my mom said his face changed to pale white. When the time came for Mitch to tell my mom about this move, my mom flipped out. Mitch and my mom were only fighting for joint custody of us, but because Hannah and John lied so much, the judge took joint custody from them and gave full custody to Mitch and my mom. They even lied about my mom's dad, my pop-pop, saying that he was gay and that we always wanted to sleep with him. We loved him. He calmly explained to the judge that it was no picnic to sleep with us. Sometimes, peeing in the bed, taking the covers, and annoying him in any way we could. Ludicrous of them.

Once Mitch and my mom got us full-time, it was the middle of the school year. Instead of taking us out of school and going to a new school, Mitch would drive us about 45 minutes each way to take us to school and home. It was especially bad for me because I would get carsick every single day. To make things even worse, Brady was not doing well in school. Mitch had to get Brady to school earlier to meet with his teachers. Somehow, Brady made the dean's list that year. He went from barely passing to being on the dean's list. This is an excellent example of what living with the correct parents can do for you. Luckily for me, I was always exceptionally good in school! I loved the challenge of it. Like a game of chess, the longest chess game that every child must go through and how you do this chess game determines your future for the most part.

The first firm memory I have of living with Mitch was the first time I ever got carsick and vomited. I'm not sure where we were coming from, but Mitch stopped at a gas station on our travels, probably from school. I played Pokémon in the car the entire time Mitch stopped to get gas, but I was very sick from the drive and playing Pokémon the whole drive. Immediately when we stopped, I started puking all over Mitch's nice new Jeep. I could not wait a few seconds to get out of the car. I just couldn't wait. That's when I learned I could no longer play games or read in the car. Since that day, I've been struggling with carsickness. Thanks to the genes I inherited from my mom.

As I said before, Mitch first signed me up for basketball when I still lived with John, which was incredible because it was the first time I had played organized sports. My first early passion became basketball, and I quickly fell in love with the sport. According to Mitch, we were such sissies when we came to live with him and my mom that the first thing he did was sign us up for Little League football. I was unsure how Brady thought about it initially, but I loved it. Thanks to this, I made a lot of friends who would be close friends of mine until I graduated high school. Even though Brady and I were so sheltered until this point, we had no trouble making friends. Even though our earlier living situation sheltered us, we went to school every day. We learned valuable social skills when we were free to roam outside the basement. Eventually, one day, we were rebaptized denominational Christians with my Uncle Billy, my mom's brother in Philly. The pastor is one of my favorite people. I still watch his sermons most Sundays. This is where our lives really began with our real dad, Mitch.

3

The Formative Years

We were living in Hampstead, Maryland. It was a nice town, with very nice people and hardly any crime. I had just started at Hampstead Elementary School. It was interesting because it was a completely new school with new people in a new town. The first person I met was the son of the people who had the house before us. He was one year younger than me but a cool dude. I was invited to his birthday party at a roller-skating rink. I had never been to a skating rink before, and I thought it would be fun, which it was at first. Once I put the skates on, everything changed. My fun at the party came to a rapid end. When I lived with John, I had terrible balance, and Brady picked up using his body much quicker than I. Since I was not allowed to play sports or do anything athletic, especially balance-related, I had no idea how to use my body except for basketball thanks to Mitch. I took one single step onto the slick rink, and I fell and broke my leg, my tibia. I was going to be the new kid in school with a broken leg and crutches. It did work out well for me because, on the first day of school, a friendly kid felt sorry that I had a broken leg and was a new kid on crutches. He felt sorry for me, and we quickly became best friends. His name is Zack, and he is a very talented athlete.

I wanted to be more athletic and coordinated. My friends and I called Zach "Sack" in high school after the movie Wedding Crashers came out. In that film, they call the Zach character "Sack" the whole movie.

I had this conversation with Sack during high school; is it "discoordinated" or "uncoordinated"? Regardless, that was me my entire life. I've always enjoyed working hard on improving things and watching the improvements. It came easy for me. It happened in basketball and football as well. I love basketball a lot, but I think my heart was always in football the most because there was a fear combined with the athletic component, which I thought was cool. Not many exciting things happened between middle school and high school, but I made many great friends, met my favorite football coaches, and started my long journey through braces. Braces lasted until my first or second year of high school.

My teeth were a huge mess. Thank God I had some great orthodontists in my area and an awesome stepdad who cared enough about me to spend all that money for me to get a beautiful smile. It was around 8th grade when I quickly became addicted to working out. My mom had an excellent trainer named Dani K, and now she has her gym. Every day after school, she would come to our house to teach me how to work out correctly and train me intensely, which I loved. We quickly became very close friends for life.

My teeth and jaw were not great, so the orthodontist put in some crazy contraption in my mouth called the Herbst. It felt like having hydraulics in my mouth. It never felt great, but it was well worth the pain. No pain, no gain. It fixed my jawline immensely! It made me a lot more attractive, which I greatly appreciate.

Brady was on my same team when I played my first few seasons of Little League football, but it was because they used body weight to choose what league you played in. Brady was always skinny and light, so he played in the same league as me, where most people were my age. Brady was by far the best player on the team. It is called being older but lighter. He was a very gifted defensive lineman. He was very athletic, quick, and strong for his age. Around that same time, Brady started to get very into skateboarding, and eventually, he gave up football to focus on his love for skateboarding and getting great at it. When he fell in love with skateboarding, I fell in love with football. My closest friends in middle school were Cory from the football team,

Kenny K., Sack, and Nick Strong. Nick Strong did not go to my middle school. I met Kenny from classes and Cory from the football team; his dad was our coach. He was an excellent coach. The best head coach I ever had.

Nick Strong was my first best friend of my short life, excluding Brady, of course, but Nick Strong was a best friend who was not family. I met him in elementary school. He was not the dude that felt sorry for me; that was "Sack." It worked out famously because he became one of my best friends during my upbringing. He's the whole reason I met Nick Strong because Nick Strong and Sack were already great friends; he had introduced me to Nick by the time I was in fifth grade. Nick Strong and I had become best friends for life too.

Since Mitch made a lot of money with the business that he started, we had a large and awesome house. Nick Strong and I would spend the weekend with Brady, Devin, and baby Shane at our house. Nick said my family would practically take him in on the weekends. We also had large summer parties with all our friends and some of Brady's. Nick was the only one of our friends who roller skated, unlike Brady and his friends who skateboarded, but everyone liked Nick because he was always the nicest person. Brady and his friends always aimed to convert him to skateboarding, which he eventually did. Even beyond our friendship, our families continued to get close. Somewhere along the line, we realized that my uncle Billy and Mar Mar, Nick's aunt, were involved in the same church in West Chester/Downingtown, PA. We later discovered that Nick's dad, Mar Mar, and my mom grew up in the same neighborhood. They already knew each other—small world. Even though we ended up going to different middle schools, with me going to Shiloh Middle School and Nick going to North Carroll Middle School, we remained very close friends. We would still spend a lot of time together on the weekend. Even on some school nights, Nick would stay overnight at my place, and my mom would drive him to his middle school in the morning. We were that close. Almost every Friday night, from elementary to middle school Nick, Sack, and others would always go to the skating rink and try to 'mac on' or flirt with girls a year older than us. We failed 100% of the time. Nonetheless, we would try every weekend for years on end. Upon entering high school at North Carroll High School, we were all reunited again. All from North Carroll and Shiloh Middle Schools, respectively. Except for Sack, who went to Delone Catholic High for one year before transferring to North Carroll High School the following year. This was where we came of age, proverbially made our marks, and grew up.

We all witnessed each other getting our first girlfriends, falling in love, getting broken hearts, and fighting about petty things we'll never remember. We spent a lot of time trying new things, failing, and learning, generally being teenage boys. My house was always the epicenter of our coming of age. We spent countless nights at our first house, always watching the Ravens games with Nick's dad and other family friends and just friends. I loved the first house; it had everything a growing boy would ever want. A pool, a pool house, a treehouse, a basketball court, a stream and family members even built a half pipe together for us for skateboarding. As I got older and more into football, I wanted to get bigger and stronger so I could get better and more athletic, so my parents made a nice workout area for us to use with Dani, my mom's incredible trainer, who taught me everything about working out correctly. My favorite thing about the house was the hot tub outside on the deck—maybe the best part of the house. We had some great times at this house with fabulous family parties.

Mitch's business was crushing it for many years, so he decided to make a significant change and build his own house in the same town. Around my 11th-grade year, we moved to our new house, which was larger and nicer than the first.

This house had more amenities to enjoy, including a bigger pool with a fantastic home gym, sauna, playroom, oversized shower in the basement, right next to the sauna, a pool table, dartboard, pinball machine, basketball hoop with a light above it, and a big projector in the basement, which eventually became Brady's bedroom. There was even a lift for working on cars in the outside garage, with an apartment above that garage. To make things even cooler, an apartment was built above the outdoor garage for my pop-pop to live with us. We spent countless nights at the new house having Nerf wars, playing basketball, skateboarding, night swimming, and trying to get girls in the sauna with us. Brady and all his friends would party and drink, but none of my friends drank. My friends and I started drinking years later, but I only drank after my first year of college. Regardless, we still always had fun together without alcohol, always trying to stay strong in my Christian values.

Also, in my high school days, Mitch bought a beach house in Ocean City, Maryland, which was awesome. It was very close to the beach, and it was right on the water on the bayside. For those unfamiliar with Ocean City, Maryland, it's a sweet beach town between Delaware and Maryland. On one side is the Chesapeake Bay, and then there's the Atlantic Ocean on the other. Here we would spend a lot of time in the summer at that house with the whole family and always with some of Brady's friends. In Maryland, the big thing once people graduated from high school was going to the beach for a week at the start of the summer, called senior week, in Ocean City, MD. All the seniors would party, drink a lot, and hook up with each other. Brady made such a giant mess of the house during his senior week with his friends that we couldn't stay at the beach house for our senior week. I don't remember any memories of my senior week, and I didn't drink at all.

Besides my immediate football friends in high school, I had many other great friends at that time. I may forget some people, but they included AJ and his whole family and many others. During high school, I enjoyed meeting and making friends with everyone I possibly could. This desire to meet and befriend everyone I met may have come from my inability to have any friends until I could live with my mom and Mitch, where Brady and I were finally able to. This aspect of my personality has never left me, and I thank God.

I don't remember being very shy at any point in my life; I think I only got less shy as the years passed. I became far less shy when I moved in with my mom and Mitch. In high school, I became close friends with many friends in various groups. I love meeting people, with me being more of a jock with the closeness of my friends, who are very into different sports, mostly the football team. We had a massive group of friends throughout the school from different grades, both younger and older. If I remember correctly, I first met Nick Berry of the Berry family in high school. He was Brady's age, or one year younger, which is how Brady and I met him. Nick Berry has a younger brother named AJ, who is one year younger than me. It didn't matter that he was younger; he had a great, funny, and fun personality, so much so that he and many of our friends became close, especially with Nick Strong and me. I made it my mission in high school to be friends with everyone I could and would be able to speak to. Maybe because I was not allowed to have friends in my early childhood, or perhaps that's just my personality.

AJ and Nick were outstanding soccer players, with AJ being the better. I'm sorry, Nick. Soccer is AJ's passion in life like mine was football during this time in my life. Their whole family has dark brown hair, and they are all good-looking. From the oldest son to the youngest, the daughter. Also, they are all short—the whole family—like a little under average height. AJ is a very kind person with a good attitude, so I enjoyed spending time with him. He became a large part of my life and my whole friend group. It became a kind of weekly thing where I would go to their house for dinner once a month or so, which is how I became close with the whole family except their oldest brother, Will, who I only met once or a couple of times but is a good man and he had a son of his own. AJ also has a nice younger sister, Serra. I would always make inappropriate jokes about her and me, playing "hopscotch," if you know what I mean. The family knew it was all in love.

His parents are both very relaxed and fun to hang out with. His mother, Holly always wanted to make food for me, and his father, John loved cooking on the grill for us all the time. John worked as a construction guy, and Holly ran a daycare in town. I must have made an excellent first impression with their family because eventually, after my last few years of high school, or even after high school, I would still go over to AJ's house for dinner, maybe monthly, especially on the weekends, whether AJ was there or not. It was curious that his parents loved me so much, having four children of their own, but I enjoyed them and the family each time I visited them. It was very easy since their house was very close to my house in Hampstead, Maryland; they lived in Manchester, the nearest town to Hampstead, probably 10ish minutes away.

AJ's mom was a great friend to me; she could tell that I was kind of lost in my life, and she always wanted to help me with the many things I struggled with throughout my life, good and bad. AJ and his parents continued to be great friends of mine as I ventured into the different places my life would eventually take me. This family's most significant contribution to me was not until much later. Again, we will get there.

As I continued my life in various ways, I kept the family in my heart. I had a great friend, Tony, whom I still talked to from high school. What an incredible friend! It's partly because of Tony that I am still here to tell this story.

The only people I talked to more than Tony were Brady, Nick Strong, and Zauhn, an incredible man I will talk about later. Talking about my high school days, Nick Strong and I were always great friends with everyone in the school. We had no enemies because we always tried to treat people the way we wanted to be treated. I had a great time in high school, and I made many great friends inside and outside of school. Even though Nick Strong and I had some different friend groups and interests throughout high school, we would still do almost everything together in some form or fashion. Also worth mentioning, regardless of our beliefs now, is that we had a great church group which included Sack, Nick Strong, and a great Christian friend with solid faith that I always looked up to, almost as much as Uncle Billy. Jesse always put me on the right path, and I appreciate that to this day. I was always so afraid of falling away from God, so much that I quickly got caught in the position of judging others for their actions, which is only for God, not me. It wasn't very easy for me. I wanted to do things my friends would do, all while trying to live like Jesus by staying away from sin the best way I knew. I always wanted to inspire my friends to do the same. I wasn't much of a Christian though, only attending church on Sundays. Sexual sin was always my downfall. I sustained from sex for a very long time, but not from all sexual acts for now...

We began considering going to college as we entered our junior year of high school, with our sights set on the University of South Florida. However, out of the friends I applied with, I was the only one who received an acceptance letter. Before applying, we drove from Maryland to Tampa, where Nick had an uncle. Over the years, our families did a lot of vacationing together.

Every President's Day weekend, Nick Strong's grandparents would rent a large house in Massanutten, Virginia, and our families would spend the whole weekend snowboarding (which I was never good at), chilling, skiing, and eating great food. We would also play this crazy German dice game called Und Vidor. Also, we had a large Father's Day cookout with many great friends and family, always with Nick and his family. These are some of Nick's fondest memories of us together from elementary school to today. Nick has always been my best friend, and he taught me so much throughout life, and I hope I taught him too. Throughout our lives together, we never got into a fight. Nick Strong is the only one of my friends for whom Brady has nothing but praise. After being best friends since fourth grade, he's a great guy and a class act.

Upon starting high school, my favorite things about school were making friends, challenging myself each day, doing very well in my classes, and playing sports. I learned it takes practice and concentration, especially. I learned at a very early age that I was very good at learning and school; I loved challenging myself with school and sports, namely football.

When I started high school, I signed up for all honors classes because I loved the challenge and school but

I lacked street smarts. I've always loved challenges in all forms, especially when it came to my body and my mind simultaneously. My first two years of high school were casual. I met new friends, kissed a girl or two, and did very well on my freshman and JV football teams. I was never the biggest, strongest, or fastest, but I was good at pushing myself and working hard. I was one of the starting cornerbacks on the football team both years. One of the coolest things that happened when I was a junior in high school—though I'm not sure how it happened—was that somehow, I talked one of the best-looking girls in the school into being my girlfriend. It was a big deal because I was never one of the most attractive guys in school. She was even one year older than me. It didn't last long. Instinctually, I did not fight it. Hence came my senior year, with trouble in the form of football.

As a result of wanting to be the best player I could be, I worked out a lot more the year before my senior season started. I gained a lot more muscle from it. I was a lot stronger and faster as a result. I prayed every night and tried to live like a Christian, knowing God would always protect me throughout my football career. As much as Uncle Billy and a great Christian friend named Jesse always tried to help me grow my faith, I never really felt a very strong relationship with Jesus at this point in my life. I knew I was always protected and loved, but I don't think I ever did my part to create a relationship, aside from just going to church on Sunday and praying before bed. I was young, naïve, and lukewarm. My parents will tell you that I thought that I was better than others or holier because I didn't drink or have sex. I'm just now getting or trying to get past that trait, my naivete. I had to change my whole life. I always wanted to think everyone was good and had the best intentions, but I've learned in my travels that, sadly, that is not always the case.

The summer leading up to my senior season, I got in contact with a football trainer and a few friends, and I would go and work out with him almost every day. We met this trainer because he would come to our field at our school a few days every week and train the whole team. My teammates and friends who attended the training daily would drive about 35 or 40 minutes each way. I could not drive yet, so I rode with a friend who could. We had become far better players by the time our season started. Subsequently, due to the training and gains, I was moved from cornerback to outside linebacker, which I couldn't have been more excited about. I mean, that's the whole reason I worked out so hard all summer. I became a very hard hitter in the weeks to come.

When the first scrimmage came, I was so incredibly pumped I couldn't contain myself. We first played against a team we had never played, and they were very good. I was very prepared. That was my first time going head-to-head with a large opposing lineman, and I loved every second of it. It hurt so good, hitting and sacking the opposing quarterback and tackling running backs. This has been my passion since I started playing football. Somewhere amid that game, I experienced the first-ever stinger of my life. For those who don't know what a stinger is, sometimes called a burner, here is the Google definition: "Injuries that occur when the nerves of the neck and shoulder are stretched or compressed after an impact. These injuries are common among contact and collision sports and are named for the stinging or burning pain that spreads from the shoulder to the hand." I think I had at least two in that scrimmage alone. I had no idea what was happening, so I played on. It did not feel great, but I had worked for this my whole high school career, so I was not going to let a little pain stop me. In the famous words of my uncle Daddy Matt, "stop being a little b****," I continued the season, but it kept happening.

Since I was playing and playing well, our athletic trainer for the school could see how much I loved playing the game and how much it meant to me. She told me I could keep playing, but one more stinger and my season would end. At this point, I had recorded six sacks of the quarterback in this early season. I was doing great in this new position and doing everything I could to prevent this last stinger for as long as possible. I tried everything, including getting bigger and more intense neck protection pads, bigger shoulder pads, different types of neck braces for shoulder pads, more parts for my shoulder pads, bigger shoulder pads, and even getting pretty girls to massage my shoulder and neck, but no dice. It was all a futile attempt. In the third game, it came. After my first couple of stingers, I was no longer allowed to practice, so my body and neck were being saved for the games. During game #3, week three, one final stinger came, and I had to stop playing football. Doctor's orders. This was devastating for me. My dream has always been to play college football. This looked very unlikely now. My first life dream was taken away.

Once I finished playing for the season, I had constant pain in my left upper body, stemming from my neck and shoulders to my whole left hand. I got to the point where my left hand was completely numb with pins and needles all the time for weeks. Since I was in so much pain, I went to physical therapy for my neck and shoulder; they worked wonders on my pain and injury in time. I was also experiencing some crazy amounts of sleep paralysis. To anyone who has ever experienced this, it's terrifying. I would be dreaming, and then, out of nowhere, I would have no control over my body anymore, like I was paralyzed both in the dream and in real life. Hence, sleep paralysis. Then I would go back to sleep. This would happen to me over the next few years, but not nearly as frequently. By the time I was in college, it had disappeared entirely. If it did happen, it would dissipate much quicker. The stingers happened because my neck was too weak to take on the impact of the hits. I would hit people with my head by accident in football too often, with my neck being too weak and the surrounding muscles.

When I finished playing football, I was in constant pain throughout the day, every day during school. Thankfully, I had a great friend who had some leftover prescription ibuprofen that he graciously shared with me during my time of angst. I no longer had a way to challenge my body like I did with football, so I was considering the Navy or something like that. I continued to challenge myself, mind, and body by waking up at 4:00 AM before school every day and going to the gym, working out, and then swimming, learning the combat sidestroke if I was going to be in the Navy. This was the first time I was thinking about my future. My before-school workouts also gave me more time to do other things after school. I thought that would be a good fit for me. I talked with a recruiter for the Navy, and I was told that because of my neck injury, I would not be a good fit for the military. Still, I was getting into swimming at my favorite gym 4 Seasons Sports Complex, in Hampstead, MD. I would swim as cardio after my workout. Careless of the fact I couldn't play football anymore, as was my dream to play in college. I still wanted to find a way to push my body and mind daily. I was blessed with such hard-working determination that I was desperately searching for a way to use it, and I was lost with no direction at all anymore with what to do after high school. Little did I know the grandeur of what God had before me.

As a senior in high school, I took AP biology and AP

Spanish classes for the challenges, respectively. I also took German I because 'why not?' I never knew what I wanted to do with my life after high school. I always dreamed of playing football in college, but that did not sound too great for me anymore. So, after my senior year of high school, I decided to go to school somewhere different to experience different ideas, people, and places. As a result of my excellent academic standing, I was never rejected by any of the colleges to which I applied. I felt that the world was my oyster. My closest friend from high school was my best friend Chris Martin, whom everyone always called Flutie. I think I met him when we were freshmen in high school, and he tried out for quarterback on the football team. He was so incredibly short, like Doug Flutie. All the seniors loved him because of his hilarious personality and short stature. Eventually, everyone started calling him Flutie and it stuck. It's especially funny now because Flutie is about the same height as me. Still, some people call him Flutie. I got incredibly close to him over our high school days, so much so that we decided to go to college together. We were slightly lost with how our lives would go and how to get there. I guess my first mistake was never thinking about my future at all. My goals and my dreams were constantly changing for me. I never had an idea, but God decided for me—you will see later.

4

Carroll Community
College

When deciding on a college, I had a great conversation with Flutie about Hawaii. Flutie had a friend in Hawaii who spoke highly of it, so I applied to the University of Hawaii and was accepted. With excellent grades and finances, I thought, 'why not?'

Every summer, I would go to my uncle's farm in Virginia and work with him for at least a week. Daddy Matt, or Uncle Matt, had a fantastic organic and heirloom vegetable farm with incredible taste and appearance. It was hard work, but worth it, if only for the laughs each time I worked with him. He knew it was a learning process for me to grow as a man and closer to the whole family. I always enjoyed experiencing the different ways of life there. It was a departure from the easy life I had every day at home. I needed to leave my comfort zone and experience some hard work for a week. Not just the hard work, but the hilarious insults—his specialty. Memorable times mixed with hard work, dealing with tomato hornworms, bug squashing, guaranteed bags under my eyes, exposure to excessive poison (oak or ivy), and enduring embarrassing jokes at my expense that we'll laugh at for ages. I have a lot of family in the West Virginia/Virginia area. I loved those weeks of spending quality time with my extended family, which was always great. These are memories I will cherish forever.

When I decided to move to Hawaii for school after the first semester of my freshman year at Carroll Community College, Daddy Matt finally paid me for my years of work at the farm. I was always very good at saving money, which made life a little easier. After high school ended, I had no challenges in my life except for always working out. Flutie and I decided to go to Carroll Community College, graduate with our AAs, and then transfer to Hawaii. That was the plan, anyway. Again, my lack of patience got the better of me.

A high school friend told me, "patience is a fruit chew," but I already ate mine. That's what my life has always been. It was a close friend from middle to high school, a hilarious individual who was consistently one of the strongest students on the football team and the entire institute.

In the first year after high school, I became much more interested in working out, and it consumed my whole life aside from school. The fact that my friend was always the strongest kid I knew by far led me to suspect that he had helped me become so strong. Eventually, in my freshman year of college during the summer I finally had a deep conversation about his first experience with steroids in high school. He told me all about how he got medicine to prevent the inevitable acne. He had a thorough understanding of how to use the right vitamins and supplements to prevent the liver, among other organs and body parts, from suffering harm from steroid pills. There is a lot you must know to take steroids correctly. Thankfully, I had a friend who knew all the ins and outs of the whole process. I don't remember the process we went through when we first ordered them, but it was not difficult. I do remember that much. I ordered them to my house in Maryland and they arrived without problem.

The family had a cleaner for the house, and this man's name is Mark, a great guy. I distinctly remember when the small package came with the pills inside. Mark was perplexed as to why I had a package from Moldova, the country where the pills came from. I simply covered it by saying that it is a sponsor-a-child thing. Not a great cover-up, and I'm sorry for lying. He was super helpful and a hard worker, and he helped Shane with his homework daily. We always had good conversations. When he had his son, he would take him to our house too, and it was awesome.

The pills were not too expensive; my friend and I split the cost. We each took half of the pills after doing a lot of research before they were shipped. The weirdest thing about the whole undertaking was how they arrived; in a tiny package, a small envelope with no letter inside, but instead, there were two little pieces of masking tape securing the pills inside. It's kind of weird but also genius. That's an intelligent way to get past customs. So, props to them.

We both started taking them right when they came in the mail, with the correct precautionary measures. Gosh, did they work! It was the first time I realized why people use them—because they work. I noticed a significant difference on the first day of taking them. It was as if I could exercise indefinitely without experiencing any fatigue. We did a lot of research before we ever got them. We chose the type of steroids that cause the fewest side effects. There were some side effects, but not nearly as many as the more potent varieties. The first one I noticed was that my acne was getting slightly worse, which is to be expected. The two worst side effects I experienced were how fat my face got and the extraordinary number of wet dreams I experienced throughout the time, and maybe one year after. They slowed down after the pills were finished. It wasn't very pleasant, but to be expected. I was working out my neck a lot during these steroid workouts, considering that my neck needed a lot of muscle strengthening for injury prevention. My neck became so big that Nick Strong said that my neck looked like a penis, whatever that means. I know that steroids are harmful to use, but the strength I obtained from my use of them in my late teenage years came into play for me later in my life in a big way—but I'm getting ahead of myself again.

I thought if I were to strengthen my neck and body enough, I could find a way to continue trying to play college football. I couldn't fully let go of this dream until I knew I had tried all the possible avenues.

There was a large and athletic black dude at my home gym in Hampstead, 4 Seasons Sports Complex, that I would always see. He looked around my age, but there were not many black people in my small town, and he was incredibly strong and happy at the gym. Eventually, I decided to meet him since we were always there at the same time. Somehow, I learned that I played football against him in high school. I could tell from how hard he always worked out that he had been training for college football. At this point in my life, my dream had not yet changed. In talking with him, I learned that his name is Zauhn. I knew I had lost my chance to play football in college with my neck injury in high school, but I would not give up so easily. I thought if I strengthened my neck enough with the help of these steroids, I could talk a coach into giving me a chance to play again with a much stronger neck that kind of looked like a penis.

As I talked to and worked out with Zauhn, we realized we both had the same goal: to become the best athletes and football players. It was only a short time until we became everyday workout partners and ultimately became lifelong friends. From the moment I introduced myself, we immediately hit it off. We had a lot in common, both loving to push our bodies. Our days revolved around training and trying to save and make money, especially since the summer was his last chance to make some money before starting his first year of college playing Division One football at Colgate University. He met a speedy man at church, Mr. Romaun, who agreed to help in his training with all his experience in speed training. After we became training partners, Mr. Romaun also agreed to train me. Each day of that summer, after our shift as camp counselors at the gym's summer camp, we would work out with strength training and then meet Mr. Romaun for workout number two: speed training.

Later, we started training with another guy named CJ, who was at least one or two years younger than us but incredibly fast. Zauhn and CJ always won the races, which was okay. I was never the best, most athletic, or fastest, but I always worked hard. That was my athletic gift—working hard. CJ was also a very gifted lacrosse player, with lacrosse being his favorite sport. Regardless, I think he loved the challenge in all sports, maybe just being the best possible, no matter the pain accrued, like both of us. It became a regular routine for us to pick CJ up, train hard with Mr. Romaun, drop CJ off, and then eat a nice dinner with his family. CJ had two attractive older sisters and a little brother. It was a great, fun, and funny Christian family. The oldest sister is a pretty, young lady for whom I had an affinity, but I was just never ready to have a girl in my life yet. We liked each other, and we were attracted, but I was too preoccupied with training and my goals. It's all good because she eventually found her suitable Romeo. Now she is happy and married to the love of her life, and I'm happy for her.

The first year that Zauhn and I trained together to make a little money for my life and Zauhn's college football and school year, we started a small grass-cutting business in his vast neighborhood. We called this small business Zauhn's Lawns and did it on the weekends. We made some walking-around money, which was especially nice for him during school. We did it at least two years throughout his career. Zauhn got the idea because he already had many grass-cutting supplies, including a lawnmower and weed whacker. Zauhn's job on every lawn we did was the lawnmower; mine was to get the weeds with the weed whacker. I will never forget the first lawn we ever did. It was a very old lady's house and gosh, it had not been cut in at least a year. We had our work cut out for us, for sure. Though it was hot and demanding and took a long time, we pushed through it and got it done. We never had a yard quite as tricky or overgrown again, which we were both grateful for. When the summer was over, Zauhn returned to Colgate University for Division One college football and to pursue an architecture degree. I enjoyed training with both, hanging out with them, and hanging out with CJ's family. It's a summer I will never forget.

After summer training, we went our separate ways. Zauhn went back to college for his freshman football season, CJ continued his high school football career, and I began my first time in college, which was at Carroll Community College. I decided to push the limits of my body with all the training and working out, especially my neck, with neck exercises/"nexercises" with every workout with Zauhn. I was finally ready to meet with the coach of this local university's first football season. I was excited to meet him at the school and see how I could help the team. This small private college was about 30 minutes from my house. At this point in my life, I didn't want to drink or party at school. Instead, I decided to learn to play the guitar. I have always loved music and thought, "Why not?" It's a hobby to keep me on the right path.

I thought that if I never told the coach about my neck injury in high school, he would never know, and I could live my dream of playing college football. Before the meeting, I prepared a meeting with him by making a video of my strength, speed, and abilities. Sadly, things didn't work that smoothly, even with the video.

I had been emailing the coach, but this was the first time that I would meet with him in person. I thought since I usually make good first impressions with the people I meet, it could be okay if I didn't tell him about my high school neck injury, and he would be none the wiser. I went into his office and met him face-to-face for the first time, and I guess at some point before our meeting, he was informed of my high school neck injury. He proceeded to give me the bad news that he and the school couldn't take the chance that I presented with my medical history, and that was it. My first-lifetime dream had been taken away from me fully. Regardless, I loved all the training with Zauhn and CJ to prepare me for the letdown. God had different plans.

I wouldn't change it for anything, especially with all the lifetime friends I made, especially Zauhn. To this day, he is still one of my closest friends. Just a great all-around man! Zauhn is a friend who never leaves, no matter what happens. I have a few of those friends. This was the first significant change in my plans since my adult life began. It was tough looking back, but I've always been a survivor. I just had to change my plans, which was a bad change for me then. Now that I was not getting ready for the football season, I had to find another way to spend my free time. It all worked out. I realized that my football career had ended entirely. I started playing the guitar more and more every day. I had loved music from an early age and more as time passed. I very quickly found myself enthralled by it. Luckily, Brady was pretty versed in the guitar from his high school days, when he played in and started a band. He taught me the basics at the start.

I was itching to take my life somewhere new for the first time. Flutie and I decided we wanted to go to the University of Hawaii for our real college experience after graduating from community college. I've always been awful at showing patience, and it has gotten me into trouble over the years. It's something I'm working on. I was so bad with patience that I couldn't wait. Instead of graduating from Carroll, I enrolled at the University of Hawaii with excellent grades after my first year at Carroll Community College. I packed up my clothes and went to Hawaii with the help of my mom and Brady. It was an excellent vacation for all of us. To make things even more incredible for me when I first experienced college, Flutie was visiting his friend in Hawaii simultaneously. This helped me meet people because we are a great team. It was fascinating, and it was easy to meet people.

The first person I met while with Flutie, going to get my schedule for the semester, was a dude doing the same. I found out that he was my next-door neighbor in my dorm. His name is Jake. Before he started at the University of Hawaii, he was a sponsored snowboarder in Bend, Oregon. He stopped this career because he had too many concussions throughout his career. I could tell because he spoke slowly, and he was cool. His roommate was another great friend named Nam, a little Vietnamese dude from Northern California. My roommate was a local from Maui, one of the other islands in Hawaii. I have no idea whether he truly despised me or found it amusing to ridicule me for various reasons; nevertheless, I invariably relished his company.

My closest friends at the University of Hawaii were all from Massachusetts, not from the same town, but close. They were not friends and had never met before going to Hawaii. My closest guy friends were named Ian and Justin. Ian came to Hawaii with his girlfriend Julia. Similarly, Justin moved to Hawaii with his girlfriend, Emily. Emily went to the university, but Justin worked at a nearby hotel. She and I became incredibly close throughout my short time in Hawaii. It's funny because Justin and I also became great friends, even though they broke up soon after coming to Hawaii together. Also, Ian and Julia had broken up before or after coming to Hawaii. That did not stop them from spending the whole time I was in Hawaii in our close-knit friend group. This group included Emily, Ian, Justin, Nam, Jordan, and sometimes Jake and me. We had such a great time and awesome friends and family; we did everything together.

My best friend was Ian, and we became great workout partners. A lot of great conversations would come out over our workouts. I was the one who taught him how to work out. I wonder if he ever thinks about me. I regressed since Ian and I both had unlimited meal plans, so we decided to contest to see who could gain the most weight, which I eventually won, though this was not good.

As far as my classes, I took a calculus class, which was easy for me, but the teacher had a crazy accent, so I couldn't hear most of what he was saying. Still, I did incredibly well in that class. It was also challenging because I sat beside Emily, whom I was very into. My favorite class was one called Intro to the World's Religions. That was by far the most exciting class I took. It was even more interesting and my professor was Islamic. I'm sure I had at least one other class, but I don't remember the other classes. I remember spending a little time in my dorm studying and doing homework. Of course, it's been a long time since I was in Hawaii, being 31 now. I think a memory I will never forget is carving pumpkins together on Halloween. Instead of a pumpkin, I tried carving a pineapple because, Hawaii. Though I'm not a great artist, I had to try. It came out pretty good—better than I expected.

Around Thanksgiving time, I felt like I should go back home. Shane was growing up, and since we had always been incredibly close, I wanted to be able to cheer him on as he was playing high school basketball and other sports. After talking with my friends, my family, Emily, and the whole friend group, I decided I should finish this semester and return to Maryland. Before I left, Emily made me an awesome going-home dinner party with all our friends. I made the poor decision to get drunk for the first time. That, for sure, made her upset and my actions were not very kind to her. It was upsetting to me, and I regretted it. It was the last time I would ever see Emily, the first girl I felt so strongly for in my short life. I decided not to let her know how I felt because of the situation we found ourselves in. To me, it made more sense to, in the words of Uncle Billy, "leave it go," which I did. I was terrible with girls back then. I know it may be a little creepy, but a year or two ago, I was a little curious to see where her life took her, so I searched on the internet. As she was a pretty and intelligent girl, I figured I could find her or something about her life, and by golly did I. I found that she had become an influential lawyer in California somewhere. So, she did very well. As far as I know, I think Ian might still be in Hawaii. He loves it there. I know that Justin now has a kid and is married. Justin and I still talk; I should call him. I still have a few friends from that very short time in Hawaii. I finished my semester with straight A's, which was not too hard.

So, I went back to Maryland and continued my degree in general studies because I had no idea what to do with my life. I would continue attending Carroll Community College with Flutie, Tony, and Jose. Jose was the third of our trio of besties. Jose was from South Carroll High School, about 30 or 40 minutes from Flutie's high school and me. I met Jose when I first started at Carroll before I went to Hawaii, but we became closer and closer as time went on. Since I always wanted to be a good influence for Shane growing up, I told my friends not to cuss around him. With this in mind, we decided to use the word "flake" in place of the f-word. I never felt comfortable using cuss words anyway.

Flutie and I had a great time at Carroll Community College, and we got very involved with the activities at
the school, thanks to Flutie. I do not remember how we first
met the people in the Student Life office if it was my, Flutie's, or Jose's work but I'm thrilled we did. The whole time
we were not in class, we would spend all our time in that office with the fabulous ladies who worked there. That's how
we met Jose hanging out in that office. We all became close
friends after meeting at that office with the great ladies who
worked there. Our closest friend in that office was a lady
with the most incredible sense of humor we always loved
being around, named Jeana. Though we always called her
Poverty Woman, since she was doing this social experiment
where she would live in poverty to show the different obsta-
cles and difficulties involved with living under the poverty
line. She quickly became one of our closest friends at the
school. Thanks so much, Jose, for introducing us. My two
best memories from my time at Carroll—well, there are
many great memories. The ones that stood out the most
were two during my first year. Thanks to Poverty, this was
the first fun school function we all got involved in. This
one was a poverty simulation, which was cool and exciting.
Flutie and I had the job of running the pawn shop. Since
we were trying to have the most fun with the process, we
started selling and pawning babies near the end of the simulation. Of course, that was not allowed, but it was funny
for us. Maybe the coolest thing we did at Carroll was take a
bus trip with the school to New York City near Christmas
time, which made this trip more entertaining. I can't remember why Jose didn't come, but Flutie and I had a great
time. The reason for this trip was to see a Broadway show.
Instead, Flutie and I sculpted the tickets to enjoy the city a
little since Christmas was soon. We went to Old Navy and
walked around and saw that they had some promotion: if

we bought anything, they would take our picture and put it on the big screen in Times Square. It happened and was great. After purchasing a cheap pair of socks, we were on the big screen, immensely proud of our accomplishment. All we had to do was buy a very cheap pair of socks.

The most interesting thing I did at Carroll Community College, during my last semester. I signed up for an acting class because why not? It was an entertaining class with some interesting people and an incredible teacher. As a result of the excellent teaching and to get the experience (and a little extra credit), I acted in a little one-act play. It was a minimal production called "A Dog's Life." In my part, I played a dude walking into a dog shelter looking to adopt a dog. It was an awesome experience, and I'm proud I did it, regardless of the extra credit. I also had an awesome specch class with an incredible teacher, Coach D. He was great and had a great personality and I loved his class. I cannot remember my exact grades, but I think I had good grades. None of the classes were too challenging. I got my associate degree from Carroll with good grades. Flutie and Jose decided to go to Salisbury University near Ocean City, Maryland for a four-year degree now that we all graduated from Carroll.

Flutie was ready to attend university; he started at Salisbury University right after Carroll. He lived in the dorms with a cool roommate, which was great for him to meet new friends. During this time, I got into a quarrel with my parents because of my stupid actions in trusting some stuff that my extended family told me about my parents. I have always been highly gullible about everything that people tell me. I think that's why I liked school so much: I could believe what the teachers would say to me as fact without argument.

Mitch had a good amount of heart issues when he

started his own business because of the stress and poor diet for years. He had multiple heart attacks in my high school days to this point in the story. I had just come home from visiting my extended family, and they told me some things about my parents, which I, of course, believed. I couldn't wait for my extended family to get together to talk with my family before my lack of patience again took hold. I also couldn't wait for Mitch to recover from his intense open-heart surgery; I had to confront my parents about the things that my extended family told me. I went to talk to my mom about how she was dealing with her problems; she didn't agree with me very much. I spoke to them, and they were upset that I believed what my extended family said about them over their words. I didn't handle the whole situation well, and we decided it was better that I move to West Virginia to live with my aunt for a little while. Then, my parents would have time to process and moderate my actions. I was in my early 20s but still very much a child.

5

West
Virginia

I moved in with my aunts, Heather and Heidi sisters, and I got a job at GNC, a supplement store, and it was relatively quiet. My aunt, Heidi, had an old acoustic guitar, which I started playing with a lot. Before I moved to live with my aunts, Brady had taught me a little, but I wasn't ready to stop playing the guitar. When I moved to West Virginia, Heidi had never gotten very interested in and intoxicated with playing like I was becoming. Usually, I would sit in the back office of the GNC store and play Heidi's acoustic guitar until a customer came into the store. It made the time go by much quicker, and I had something to do during my spare time when there were no customers as I was trying to learn how to play guitar. I did start experimenting with alcohol more around this same time. There It was not much at her house except when I visited Flutie at Salisbury University. Once, my aunt gave me a bottle of absinthe (sans wormwood) to take to college to visit Flutie. I didn't have a car at this point. So, Heidi graciously let me drive her truck from West Virginia to Salisbury University. I was ready to visit him and have a nice trip to see how Flutie lived. This trip was short-lived, and I have one memory of it, and that's it. I went to Flutie's dorm for a little party, and I was not very experienced with drinking hard alcohol. I would not recommend it to those who have not gotten drunk off absinthe. It tastes awful, and it's very strong. Since my aunt got the absinthe in America, there was no wormwood in the instilling process; it didn't make me hallucinate.

I was quickly drinking too much, almost immediately into drinking it. Being a friend, Jose was telling me to slow down with the alcohol, but by that time, it was too late. I was busy working my chances with a cute girl who lived right down the hall. I was doing well with my moves with her, and then she invited me to go over to her dorm, and I agreed. I was way too drunk by the time I got to her room. I was close to getting sick. The last thing I remember is that I was in her bed with her, and she told me that she was not going to hook up with me. It was an excellent choice for her because the next thing Flutie knew, she was knocking on his door completely covered in vomit—my vomit. The next thing I knew, I was thrown into Flutie's shower with all my clothes on. Flutie threw together some clothes for me, I drank some water, and I slept through the night. Of course, I felt awful for throwing up all over their dorm room. I tried to make it up for them by buying them all pizza, which surely didn't make up for it, but I tried at least. Right? I would have tried to help clean if I wasn't so hungover. It was a little of a disappointment for me, but I imagine it was worse for them. This was my only time throwing up from alcohol.

After visiting Flutie at Salisbury, I realized that I wanted to finish college at some point. After the short visit, I decided that I was going to start my bachelor's degree at Salisbury University and that I would apply and live with Flutie and Jose. Before I could get there, I had to buy myself a cheap car—my first car. It was a Subaru Impreza, which was cheap to buy from my step-grandpa. He would always buy beat-up vehicles, fix them, and resell them for a profit. That is where my first-ever vehicle, which I purchased with my money, came from. I bought it for $2000, and it was great and lasted about two years. Not bad for two grand. It's funny though, I never once passed the emissions test in Maryland with this car. Every month, I had to get an extension and pay $15 until I got rid of the vehicle. It just became another extra bill I had to pay every month.

Once I bought that car, I was ready and packed up for Salisbury University for another try at college, living in an on-campus apartment with great friends. After the great experience I had with neck injury therapy during high school football, I decided to go to school to become a physical therapist. I signed up for a few classes I needed before starting my major classes. If I remember correctly, there was a history course, a challenging physics class, and one more class I can't remember. We made a lot of friends living at this campus housing development. It included four people per apartment. Our apartment had Jose, Flutie, me, and a random guy named Wilkerson. Although he was a bit of an outcast a video game enthusiast, he was a pleasant little dude. He was probably 5'2" or even shorter. I guess I could finally talk about what Flutie and Jose looked like. I think Flutie was around my height, which is 5'10.5", but who's counting? Flutie grew a lot between high school and college, I guess. If I remember correctly, Jose was just a tad taller than us. Jose was of Spanish descent if you cannot tell from his name. Jose was a good-looking guy with a gift with the opposite sex. He would always be with different girls weekly, and it wouldn't matter if he were attracted to them sometimes. Regardless of this fact, girls always seemed to flock to him. He wasn't bad-looking, but he was no Brad Pitt either. He's a good guy though, to me always. Jose has a good build, and he was always strong. He and I never fought, unlike Flutie and Jose. They thought were both alpha males and had to argue with each other, always wanting to have the upper hand. I may have already mentioned this, but Flutie certainly had the most incredible personality and the gift of gab. He can talk to anyone about anything. He is so great at conversing with people and making friends with a great sense of humor. That's why I've always loved spending time with him. He was always a great friend to me. I know I talked about Flutie already in my high school days. I forgot to talk about his appearance, so let me start by saying that he was always a good-looking dude in my eyes, and his great personality was always the best thing about him. He always made me and anyone around him laugh every time he spoke. For that reason, girls loved him because he always made them laugh. He had good style too which I always lacked. I always got my style from my friends and Brady. He had a very distinct thing about him that somehow never bothered him as much as it would bother me if I were in his shoes, but Flutie was born with a substantial birthmark on his upper lip, which he had multiple surgeries to fix. Sadly, they never fully fixed the problem. Regardless, it never stopped him from being a great dude with a great personality and the best sense of humor that girls loved. Of course, most people would think it would be difficult for him to find girls with his birthmark, but I got to believe that it never bothered him at all. Combined with his funny personality, I couldn't respect the guy more. That could be why I became best friends with him when I first met him and now, to this day.

My time at Salisbury University was very short-lived. Not too much happened, except I made some good friends and did okay in school, minus physics class, which was the only C I received in college. This was the most challenging class I had at any college I attended. This could be a result of my significant increase in alcohol consumption over those days; I can only speculate. Whatever the case, I made some great friends at Salisbury University during my very short time, especially with the girls who lived right upstairs from us at our apartment.

I don't remember exactly how we met them, but I'm sure I was introducing myself to all the neighbors with Flutie and Jose. We quickly became friends with that upstairs apartment. We introduced ourselves, and they introduced themselves as well. We had girls named Lala, Kiki Bubbles, and Brittany with no nickname. I'm sure you could tell who the odd girl was in that apartment. Since Lala, Kiki, and Bubbles all had very similar personalities, Brittany didn't. Regardless, they got along very well with all of us, too. I always had terrific conversations with all of them, and I would visit their room when bored. Bubbles and I became the closest. I think that was because Bubbles and I had very similar personalities, and she was just a great person. All of them were charming and cool girls. Bubbles was a girl with good Christian values, which I had quickly forgotten.

We were all 21 at this point, so we had a good number of parties at our place together with a lot of alcohol. We always had our neighbors come and enjoy the festivities. Speaking of being 21, it was a ritual for everyone to go to one of the bars every week on Thursday for Thirsty Thursday, which always sucked for me because I had a very early class Friday morning. Then, we always went to a different bar every Saturday night, which I certainly enjoyed more because I had no class on Sunday morning.

I don't have a ton of memories from my short time at Salisbury University, but I do remember I drank a lot of alcohol. I remember hanging out with my upstairs neighbors the most, and they had a Keurig machine that we would always drink with them very often. Our favorite was the chai latte because this was when the movie "Slumdog Millionaire" came out or when I first saw it. We would always call Bubbles our Chai runner, a slight reference to the film. If you haven't seen it, you should. It's my favorite movie.

I also made a friend named Tony, who was very tall, and he had no fear at all. I think he was around 6'8" or something. The craziest thing we did together was one day it snowed a lot, and he had a very sweet Jeep that we drove around in the snow, and he did a lot of crazy donuts, with some serious drifting through the mix of ice and snow. I was a little afraid but always felt safe with Tony at the wheel.

Back
Home

Around Christmas time, again, I could not pay for my schooling at the university, which I was heartbroken about. There was nothing I could do this time because it had something to do with my school loans, which I took out for my semester, and I could not pay for them anymore—not my classes, housing, or anything else. So, I was going back home again, which my parents were not stoked about. Sadly, I didn't have many other options at this point. It seemed that school time for me might be over. I had tried for years at three different schools and only got my community college degree. If that's not a sign, I don't know what is.

At this point, Brady was still living at home as well. He was working overnight at a grocery store and on cars. Brady, being the great brother that he is, quickly got me a job at the same grocery store working overnight because they paid more for overnight work. I did not dislike the hours. I would go to work at night, like 11 p.m., then get off work at around 7 a.m. and go to bed for a few hours, then go to the gym and play guitar. It was not too shabby.

While I was working there, Brady decided he would move to California which had always been his dream. With skateboarding as his lifelong love, Southern California was the most significant scene, and the weather is much better than in Maryland. It was a difficult time for me because I was losing my brother to the other side of the country. I was always proud of him for taking that plunge. You must push for what you are passionate about, which is what he did.

As for me, I was getting incredibly into playing the guitar. My daily routine was waking up from sleeping after work, then going to the gym, and then playing guitar until I had to get back to work again. I enjoyed every second of it. I loved learning new things with the guitar. I learned how to play my favorite songs by reading tabs. That's how I started learning more about writing and playing better.

Before Brady left for California, he taught me some stuff about playing guitar and Brady had a great friend named Kevin, who taught me stuff too.

Eventually, I continued learning by looking at tabs for my favorite songs and learning how to make incredible sounds like these bands had. I was very into the band Blink-182 and challenged myself to learn how to play the cool-sounding guitar part in the intro of the song "Stay Together for the Kids." Next, I learned my favorite song by Blink-182, "Adam's Song." My next challenge was learning how to play and sing together simultaneously. It was a little process, but I was off to the races once I got it. The first song I learned was "Teasing to Please" by the band Cute is What We Aim For. The second was the song "Approach the Bench" by the Audition. Then, most of the time I spent on music was spent writing and recording my ideas. A friend, Kyle, and I would get together for writing and playing once or so a week, but he was a busy dude. Nick Strong was working on his college career, but Nick has an older brother, the same age as Brady, with whom I played football. We were always good friends. Nick also had a little sister named Sami, a great person and friend—the whole Strong family.

As I was saying, Nick's older brother was an incredibly hard worker in anything that he did. Athletics, school, and his hobbies. His name is King, but everyone calls him Mike. He was a freaking awesome guitarist. Mike and his roommate at college were both very talented guitarists, and they had always wanted to be in or start a band together. I'm glad they did because my first band would never have been if they hadn't. Mike's roommate was another super great dude named Eric, with whom I also played football in high school. So, we knew each other very well. They were two very talented guitarists looking for a bass player and a cool dude who played drums. I think Nick Strong talked to his brother and told him that I had gotten into the music world and that I could play bass in the band. I was not the best bassist, but I knew enough by this point.

My aspiration to form a band with some friends who were extraordinarily talented musicians was materializing. The next step to starting my band life was to meet with the band for the first time and to meet the drummer, a great dude named Nick M. He was from the same county as me, about 35 to 40 minutes from my house. We would always play at Nick's house because it is a pain to pack up the drums and because Nick's parents are super cool with all the noise. They would usually go out while we were playing most of the time. We started by playing covers, including "The Quiet Things That No One Ever Knows" by Brand New, "Last Chance to Lose Your Keys" by Brand Knew, and "Just What I Needed" by The Cars. Before we got together in the band, I was tasked with learning those songs on bass guitar that were not too difficult or complicated to play. I picked them up quickly and spent a lot of time learning to play them perfectly before I got together with the band to jam. By the time I got together with them and met the drummer, I had started writing some ideas and songs on my own with my recording equipment. After playing the covers for a few weeks as a band, we commenced by taking a stab at writing our original ideas.

Eric had a fantastic first-song idea for an original, and I loved it! We called it "Fire Breathing Dragon." Nick M. came up with it with his very creative mind, and it fitted with the guitar feel. So, it stuck. Next, Mike Strong wrote an awesome, intricate, and beautiful song with his deep guitar acumen. We just called that "Mike's song". By this time, I would always sing along with all the songs on my iPod as I drove anywhere, I had to go alone. I realized that

I was relatively good at matching my vocals with my voice in the song, and I thought I would eventually be able to play guitar and sing in a band one day. Before I got the chance to try out to be the singer of this band, the band leaders found a singer in the form of a close friend of theirs that Nick knew from high school too. In the meantime, I was always thinking and working on my songs and thinking of a name for the band. Then one day, I had written many ideas for the band's name, and they started to like one of my names—" All We Know." We had decided. Sometime, after a few months of practice, we got our first chance to play live, thanks to our great friend from high school and Brady too. His name is Duffy.

He had a house where he went to college, and he was nice enough to let us play for him and a friend or two for us to sample what it's like to play in front of people. It was fun, we played well, and I was freaking hooked! I wanted to do this again and continue with these friends. Sadly, we never played together again. Eric and Mike soon graduated from college, and the band had died. It was okay; I grasped the situation from their eyes. It made sense. Thankfully, I knew this would not be the end of my music career as I continued to grow my ideas little by little. With around one year of guitar playing and bass playing, I learned I could start writing and recording songs sans drums, which I had no idea how to play. Sometimes, with some vocals included, my worst habit regarding my music writing is impatience, like in every aspect of my life. I should have spent far more time learning about the songwriting process and the ins and outs of my instruments the guitar, bass, and voice. If I could go back, I would learn more, but hindsight is 20/20.

While this was all going on, I was getting more and more into writing and recording my music with the recording equipment guitar, vocals, lyrics, and sometimes bass with my laptop connected to my interface using the program Logic Pro 9, starting with GarageBand before Logic. I made a little vocal room in Shane's closet with Brady's help before his move to California. There was a little shelf to put my computer on; I put my mic stand on, and we covered the walls with blankets. That way there was no echo, and it didn't make too much noise. It worked out famously, especially as I started recording my ideas on GarageBand with Brady's nice amp and his old guitar trying some vocal ideas. Later, I started playing guitar and writing with my friend, who was about 100 times better than me at the guitar, but we had a splendid time playing together and even started a song. After creating a song with another musician, I was confident I would one day start a band. Working on music with other talented artists is way too much fun.

In concert, I quickly realized I needed to make more money than just working at the grocery store overnight. I quickly found another job as an overnight security guard at a local lumber company. I can't remember how I got or found the job, but it was the greatest job ever. My job was to walk around the yard once every hour to make sure nothing had changed, and there was a small shack where I would chill until I would have to walk around again. It was nice because there was a small TV, some outlets, and a heater for when it got cold outside. I would always take my guitar to play when I was not walking around the yard. That's where I learned most things about how to play the guitar and tried different things. One of the other dudes who worked there when I wasn't there when I had to work at the grocery store also played guitar, and he left his mini guitar amp for me to enjoy. When I found this job, I continued at the grocery store two days a week, and the rest of the week, I was at the lumberyard playing guitar and writing. I worked seven nights a week, overnight for a few months.

I was getting a lot more into playing guitar, and I bought an interface that plugged right into the laptop. It went from the guitar right into the recording program. I also purchased a recording program called Logic Pro 9. I always loved writing my guitar parts more than learning how to play the guitar. It was my favorite part of playing. I took my recording equipment to the lumber yard. Thankfully for me, Brady had gotten great at playing guitar in his early high school days, and he had a band at one point. So, I always had a guitar amp to play thanks to Brady's time spent learning and playing. This amp was awesome and loud and had different programmed sounds, with my favorite being the delay effect.

I would work on my stuff all night at the lumber yard, and then after I would wake up from sleeping in the morning, I would get back to writing and learning my favorite songs by looking at tabs to learn how other bands and guitarists made different sounds. I spent a great deal of time writing my ideas, hoping to turn them into something good, but I was in love with the writing process and trying to create the best songs I could. At this point, I would always listen to music while I showered or drove. I felt like I could match the melodies and vocals. I wanted to eventually become a singer in a band where I would also play guitar. After some practice, I learned how to play the guitar and sing simultaneously. I tried out my vocal ideas, as I would write the other instruments, just not the drums. In my recording program, I also enjoyed playing with the different sounds the program had on each instrument. The first song I ever wrote or started on my own revolved around the delay effect on the guitar. At this point, I had learned to play and sing at the same time, fluently and without thought.

So, I started searching for a band to play in, but it took a lot of work to find in my small town in Maryland. I started searching for bands from anywhere. Of course, my first thought was looking for bands in California around where Brady was, and I found one. It was a great band that was looking for a singer. I had already recorded some of a new song I was working on, with some guitar I wrote. I worked on some lyrics and melodies to send to the band in southern California to see if they liked my singing. They didn't. I continued my search and met a nice dude in Jacksonville, Florida. To me, anywhere south is a better place than Maryland with the cold winters I don't love. As a little money-saving prospect, I took a train from Philadelphia to Jacksonville. It worked out great because Philadelphia is near where Uncle Billy lives. I went to Jacksonville for a few days to meet the guitarist, but we did not click. I continued my search back home. I never stopped writing and recording at my house with my recording equipment, and by this time I had at least two songs that were close to finished, minus some bass guitar, lead guitar, and all the drums. I never knew how to play the drums at all.

My uncle Billy, the pastor of the non-denominational Christ Community Church in West Chester, Pennsylvania, has always influenced me. I had much in common with him, from our love for music and sports to working out and our Christian convictions. Uncle Billy has two sons a daughter I was very close to, and my aunt Kim. I would always take a friend or sometimes go by myself to visit Uncle Billy and his family in Pennsylvania very often, especially after getting my car. That was my first long drive after getting my driver's license—a trip to his house.

I always looked up to him to help me become the best man I could be, with his Christian values first and foremost. For that reason, I didn't have sex until I was 21 because I was waiting to fall in love at least. Sadly, for me love always evaded me.

Throughout my high school days and even after, I never had difficulty getting girlfriends; I just never found anyone I fell in love with. The word of God teaches you should wait to get married to have sex, but I always wanted to at least fall in love before I had sex. Given this fact, my first time having sex was not until I was 21. Around the same time, I was exploring a chance to find or start my own band. I had waited so long because of my religious beliefs, and I always hoped I would fall in love first. Not to mention that I felt I could not trust any girl other than my mom because of how Nancy treated me, subconsciously I surmised.

Before having sex, I had always intended to wait at least until I found someone with whom I could fall in love. Before I knew it, I was 21 years old, going to bars, and still a virgin. Love was far too elusive for me to wait for. I had hoped to find a girl that I could fall in love with. I decided that I had waited long enough. Throughout my college career, I got intimate with a couple girls. Still, I never really wanted to be in a relationship with any of them except for Emily during my short period in Hawaii, but I never even kissed her. I returned to my home in Hampstead and completely lost touch with each other. When I had finished my college attempts, I had just stopped looking for love and instead looked to have the most fun possible with girls. I was excited to see what this whole sex thing was all about. I knew there was a beautiful girl I had known because she dated a friend many years before. I knew she had always loved talking to me and spending time with me all those years ago, and I knew she was always very attracted to me. I thought I had a chance to have her be my first. I think she and I started talking via text and realized that she and I enjoyed each other. I guess you must have told her that I was still a virgin, and I think that she was honored that I chose her to be my first. To me though she was nice a with a lack of a better word, deserving. She was always a sweetheart and super kind to everyone. I loved that. I thought that finding love right now was not on the cards for me, or at least not yet. I decided to start my sexual life with her. I invited her over, and the rest was history. I'm sure it wasn't too great for her, but I enjoyed it considerably. I wanted to do it again, regardless of the girl's feelings for me. Not a great attitude. I know that I didn't do things great with my sexual relationships, but that was my thinking about sex at the time. I didn't think I would find love soon, so I hooked up with girls and hoped it would find me. I started by getting back in contact with some girls I knew from high school and some lovely new girls I would eventually get close with. I started loving doing it with different girls. It is not something I am particularly proud of, but that was my early 20s, especially knowing full well that it is wrong in the eyes of God. At this point, I didn't care much. I just went on the way the world led me. I guess I thought I was in the clear since Jesus forgives my sins anyway. It was not until much later in my life that I altogether understood what it was to be a true Christian... but more on that later.

I was excited to explore this skill. I started talking to a girl I dated in high school for a short time. This is a very short but sweet girl, and I always admired her and her family. Just a good-hearted person and family. I was aware that she had recently gotten out of a long-time relationship, and I thought she would enjoy someone to talk to through the breakup. You know, like in the movies. We got together in due course, had some fun, and then went our separate ways. Again, I went back to a girl I met in high school. This maiden was another great girl a year or two younger than me. I may have just contacted her on Facebook; she was also a great person. Once more, we chilled together for a little while, but it didn't go anywhere either. I was back in the same situation as before. This went on for a time in which I felt like I was on top of the world as I was hoping to become the leader of a band which had been a dream of mine since I started my music life. Not to mention that I began trying to meet a few girls on the Tinder app too. One of the girls became a friend of mine. She is an incredible singer, too; you know who you are. I regress; I must mention this: each time I would get with a new girl without having strong feelings or sentiments for her, I would always feel bad about it. Rightly so, it was a sinful thing, and I knew that, and it always made me feel immoral at first, but it quickly disappeared, and I would go on with my day. I guess I was still a little confused about sex and what the Bible taught. I have never really investigated much at all to this point. It was just how all my friends I loved lived, and I thought this was the way to find love. If it was even on the cards for me, because even my Christian friends were exploring fornication, so I thought to myself, "What's the big deal?" Really, what's the worst that can happen? I just continued my various sexual escapades for years. Too much.

When not thinking about girls, I tried to find people to start a band with. I started with the drummer I met in my first band, which was great because, wouldn't you know it, the drummer, Nick M., was great friends with another incredible musician named Greg. He knew his way around the guitar and bass, which was awesome for me because we could get a band started with this trio. Greg was a great musician, but his best instrument was the piano. He had been playing most of his life. We could hit the ground running since I had already been writing and recording my songs with vocals, rhythm guitar, and a little bass. We would need to write the rest of the bass and all the drums. A lot of the tentative outlines were already in the works. Of course, we all would be working on all our parts together which always led to a better song, and all our personalities were very similar too; we never fought at all. Instead, we were all very focused on writing good music just a couple of levelheaded guys writing music together. We would always play, write, and practice at Nick's, the drummer's basement. It was about 35 to 40 minutes to drive, but it wasn't too bad for the incredible friends I made in the band process. It was cool because we played every Saturday, and because it was deafening, Nick's parents would go out while we played. Eventually, we started playing in Nick's basement, in my playroom, or the outside garage, depending on the weather. I don't remember why we started playing at my house instead of at Nick's, but it worked out well because we had an old drum set from one Christmas when Shane, my youngest brother wanted to learn to play drums. We could play and practice at my house or Nick's.

After we played together for a couple of months and had a couple songs completed, Nick and Greg had a friend who played in a band in their town; his name is Paul. He is excellent and a super helpful and knowledgeable musician with everything, especially with us being a new band in the area. I think Paul is the one man I know who likes music more than myself. We were getting closer to finishing our first few songs with Paul's help. At this point, we had three songs and an intro worked out. Paul was always our pre-production guy to ensure everything worked out before we went to the studio, including getting together a few ideas from other musician friends. The first thing we did with the band before recording was play a very small show—at this local snowball stand.

We were getting close to being able to record our first EP, which included three songs and an intro. Paul was the man who put together our first EP and got it recorded. Thank God for him. He had already recorded with this incredible producer named Eric Taft, who was so instrumental (pun intended) in the finishing of the songs, significantly better than we could have ever done by ourselves. The first song on the EP was something that Brady wrote and showed me for the first time when I was learning how to play the guitar, and I loved it. We called that song "New Year's Intro" because Brady first showed me that one New Year's Eve before I started a band.

We decided to call the band Danger Parker. We got the name from Greg, the bassist's best friend's Twitter handle. He died years before. His name was Parker, and he died around high school, which was very difficult for everyone who knew him. It was a nice homage to him as Greg's best friend. It was nice because Greg and Parker were very huge fans of music; they would always listen to music together. Once we figured out the band's name and finished our first few songs, we spent a free weekend together and decided to record our first EP, "Ready as We'll Ever Be." We had all the songs completed as low-quality demos on my computer, and then the producer would devise fantastic ideas for us to make them much better. He was like our fourth member of the band. As we were recording our first EP with Danger Parker, I was still working at the lumberyard overnight, which was awesome and gave me lots of time to prepare for recording. This EP had three songs that I first started and finished with the band and the producer; they were: "New Year's Intro," "Help is on the Way," "Miss Communication," and "Tracing Lines." If you go to bandcamp.com and type in Danger Parker, it should come up with all our music. After the EP came out, the first thing we did as the "full" band was record a cover with a new producer trying to get more clients; we did a cover of the song "I'll Be There for You" from the show Friends. I always forget about this one. The EP was recorded without a lead guitarist; the producer helped a lot with that aspect until we found a lead guitarist, and we recorded the "Friends" theme song with our new lead guitarist.

Since every song we recorded on the EP was written with two guitar parts, our next challenge was finding ourselves a lead guitarist for our eventual live performances. The first place I searched was on this website called band-mix.com. It was created for the sole purpose of helping musicians find bands or add to bands. I forgot about this website with which I had an account because I hadn't used it since I was first looking for a band. Luckily, I still had my account. I quickly found a person looking for a band in my area, Carroll County, Maryland. This guitarist was from the next town over, which is called Westminster, the small city right next to my town. I contacted him on Facebook and said that I found his account on the website, and I was the lead singer and rhythm guitarist of a local band called Danger Parker. Once I got his response, I sent him all our songs from the EP and challenged him to learn the lead guitar parts, which I had a recording of how to play.

I was in the process of getting a new job when the first EP was released. I got a new job thanks to Flutie. This job was at a place that sold fasteners and supplies used in many kinds of warehouses in many business types. For a while, I would work at Fastenal during the week and at the lumberyard during the weekend, but that all changed because I wanted to spend more time with my tall girlfriend, Holly. I dated her in high school, but it was much better now that we were older. She had just come out of have a long-term relationship, and I was there for her. I liked her, and she was my first adult girlfriend. It was a big deal for me. I'm not exactly sure when I stopped working at the lumberyard on the weekends and started working at Fastenal during the week, but I think it was around the same time we got the first EP. To this day, I am most proud of the first EP we did with the help of the producer. He made a massive difference with the writing and recording. Not to mention the help of Paul O'Sullivan of the Paul O'Sullivan Band. Check out his band; it's awesome!

He had us record our music with him. Now that I think about it, we should not have made actual CDs but just had the songs downloaded online, but it was still cool either way. We tried to sell a few but mostly gave them away for free. We all had little business sense.

By this time, I had been dating the tall girl for a few months and things were going great, or so I thought. It was difficult for her because she had just finished a relationship with her old boyfriend, whom she had been with for many years. I thought she really liked me for a while. We spent so much time together; there were a few months in the beginning when we saw each other daily. We spent a lot of time together. I think it was just too much and too quickly for her. I was loving it, but she was still hung up with her ex-boyfriend. Wouldn't you know it? His name is also Cody. We dated for around two or three months, and kind of out of nowhere, she decided that she wanted to end things. It was extremely trying for me because I liked her so much, but what else can one do with such emotional anguish besides composing songs about it? Which I did. This was the first girl I had sex with that I had strong feelings for.

Of my various jobs, this one had my favorite co-workers at Fastenal. From the hilarious and incredibly hard-working manager named Tim, Darren, the navy veteran with whom I became friends and spent most of my time, and the two others inside the store. One salesman named Nate was always busy, and another inside worker named Stella was sweet. This was the highest-paying job of my life to this point, with the best co-workers and better pay. What else could you ask for? My daily routine during the two years I worked at this job was like this: I would wake up from my slumber, eat breakfast, maybe coffee, make my PBJ and apple for lunch. These were the kind of co-workers I could vent to talk through things with, and always get solid advice from. That's why I worked there for two years that and the money thing. I love those guys. The whole staff was very supportive of this musical dream of mine, which indicated that they believed in me at least a little. I appreciated it every day. My job each day was to unload the truck with the orders from the previous day and then restock the shelves. My next duty was to help the manager load his truck for delivery. There was always a lot. Depending on the day and how much he had to deliver, I would go with him, or if not, I would take the other truck to do the other deliveries for the manager, more of the smaller accounts, and help the customers that came into the store. My favorite aspect of this job was that each day was a little bit different, as well as singing while listening to music in the nice trucks. Good times.

The band got a lead guitarist, and eventually we got to know each other better, played the songs together, and quickly realized that it was a match made in heaven. This dude's name is Eric, with a hard-to-pronounce last name. It was funny the first time Flutie met Eric since his last name was so difficult to pronounce. Flutie just called him Eric Holderman, just because, and it quickly stuck. He became referred to as Eric Holderman from now on. Flutie was Danger Parker's unofficial band manager and did nothing—an honorary title. Eric and the rest of the band had the same taste in music, and we all became super close friends very quickly. Eric and I became best friends as we started this journey into band life. Now that we had a full lineup, we could start playing live together, so we did immediately. Our first live show was at the small local snow-ball stand. Next, we had the opportunity to record a cover of the Friends theme song for free as a new producer's deal to score some clients. You can find this cover on bandcamp. com; type in Danger Parker. The show was minimal, and we got our first opportunity to play the EP live for fans. We played very well, and we wanted more. After a month or so. we started working on new songs, which was better because we had someone to write with who was a real guitar player and was much better than myself. The second thing we did as a full band was record a single called "Search, Search." I never dreamed I would have the opportunity to record a music video, which was an enjoyable experience. You can find this on YouTube. It was fitting because Nick had a friend who was a very talented videographer, and we did the video with his pretty sister, who played the actress in the video. It was funny, but after the video was complete, she and I went on a date, but she was not feeling me. That was the first and last date we had. There was also a pop band from my county that I was friends with; we went to the same high school.

This band had a much larger fan base than we had and was much better at advertising. This band gave us our first big break playing live at a popular and nice Baltimore bar. It was a great place for live local music. Thanks to their friends and fan base. There were a significant number of people who had come to this show, primarily for their band. It was still fun to play for so many people. From that point on, we played many more times and at many more places. We would become regulars at this bar. I remember one time we played at this bar. Few people were at this show, and each band member drank just a little too much, minus the drummer, who was always the voice of reason. We knew we drank too much before performing, and we did awful this time. The first time though, we played great, and it was so fun. We knew we didn't do great this time, so we decided to have only one drink before we played. We never made that mistake again. I'm not exactly sure how many different shows we played but we always drank one drink before and went to Denny's afterward.

We played maybe ten shows, but my favorite ones were always at Baltimore Soundstage. It was an incredible experience for us, playing at the same place we saw some of our favorite bands play, which was a humbling experience. It was sweet because before our first show at Soundstage, I learned to spin and jump while playing guitar, which was by far the most fun and my favorite part of playing live. I always wanted to ensure the fans had as much fun as I was having. Soundstage was my favorite place to play, and they had the best sound quality, from the instruments to the vocals and everything. You should also be able to find one of our videos playing live there on YouTube.

Encompassing this time, with the band, we had been writing a lot and playing live a large amount at various venues. Boy, did I love every second of it! I was single again, too after the longest-tenured relationship of my life. She broke up with me kindly and was always nice to me. It was just bad timing for us; she was not ready. I ensured I didn't say anything bad about her in the songs I would eventually write about her. I think I only sang one slightly negative thing about her throughout the album we wrote after we broke up. That one thing was not bad, but just funny. I mentioned in one song that she gave me mono at the onset of our relationship. She would be referred to as "mono girl" from this point onward. I was in bed for approximately two to three weeks with the most excruciating sore throat of my life; antibiotics were required to alleviate the symptoms. It was rough but worth it at the time. I subtly threw it into one song. I had plenty to write about now that the girl I had liked the most in my 23 years had recently dumped me. I went to work on writing and recording, working on demos to show the rest of the band to record with our incredible producer, hopefully. The band continued writing together and we decided to record a song. This little single was almost ready for the studio when we recorded the EP. Still, we had Eric Holderman finish the songs, enhanced by his superior guitar acumen. Then we returned to the producer we recorded with for the EP to record our one single on this album, "Search, Search," with the video. The other thing that helped me through this breakup was alcohol. I slowly drank vodka throughout the whole recording of the single "Search, Search" I'm sure you could still find it on YouTube unless you are reading this far into the future when technology has advanced so much that YouTube has been replaced by something different. We were getting close to being ready for the next CD. Since I was not really over the breakup by Christmas time, I thought I could swoon her back to me with a little Christmas song that I recorded by myself at my house with my computer program and the little vocal room I made in my little brother's closet. I named that Christmas song Christmas in Your Arms, which I was proud of, but Holly didn't care. At least, that was the impression I got from her response. It was just too little, too late. Still, I had a great time making it. You can find this song on YouTube under the name Cody W. Ridenour. It was a great experience I would use to my advantage later, using my computer program and interface to write and record my songs.

That Christmas season, we played a holiday showcase in Baltimore, which we were all looking forward to, even though I was still working out my feelings from the breakup. We returned to working on our new songs and were excited about a new album with our great producer. This time, instead of three songs and an intro, we recorded ten full songs on this album called "Abandon." The album is about abandoning preconceived notions about life and what it should look like.

I forgot to mention this, but after my breakup, I was depressed, and the only things that helped me feel better were running very fast after every workout and alcohol to calm my mind—not at the same time, though. After each workout, I would run as fast as the treadmill let me go, which was a 5:30-mile pace for 1 mile. I then went to Planet Fitness which had a treadmill that let me run a 4:00 mile after every workout.

I was living at my parents' house in Hampstead, Maryland, during the week because my job was still close to my parents' house. Then, I went to Flutie's apartment on the weekends. I had to experience more. Flutie lived above a bar in Baltimore City; I paid for the apartment even though I was there for half the week. We had a ball going to bars and partying. At one of these bars one night, I drank way too much and was feeling very sick. I quickly went to the bathroom, and there was a friend of Flutie's who could tell that I was hurting. Before I knew it, this friend put a tiny amount of powder on a key and told me to sniff. I did, and I immediately felt perfect again. I then called Brady about my first and last cocaine experience. Then I returned to normal life and to a different gym, Planet Fitness, where the treadmill pace went to a four-minute pace. I would run a four-minute mile after every workout for maybe a year or more. That came into play for me and my vocals in the recording process.

The most important song for me to bypass the breakup was "Pieces and Ashes" on this album. It was not the other members of the band's favorite song on the CD, but I loved it because it helped me after the breakup. It was sincere. I remember a part of the background vocals where I held a single note in the background for 30 full seconds. I could do it because I trained my lungs for so long after the breakup by running my four-minute mile daily. I did not know when I started my training for lungs that I would use it to my advantage for more than just a sadness breaker but for my singing too. While we were recording or getting ready for the recording of the full-length album, we played another show at Baltimore Soundstage. I think this one was the best we ever played. I had to do my best because Brady and some family members came to this show. Eric was having a girl he met on Tinder come to the show from far away. Since the girl had never met Eric, she wanted to go with a friend so she wouldn't be alone. Smart. She invited her friend, Abby. We played great this whole show, and after we thanked all that came to watch and got some videos, I introduced myself to the girl that Eric invited and her friend who was very friendly, funny, and attractive.

She would later tell me that after that show, she first laid eyes on me while I was in the middle of buying drinks for underage girls. It was not a great first impression. Still, I met Abby and talked with Eric and the girl friend; immediately, I was attracted to Abby. She had dark brown eyes and very dark brown hair. I spoke throughout the night with her, and ultimately, we exchanged phone numbers. She lived around an hour and a half or two hours away. I think she was digging me, and I was digging her, hoping our paths would cross again one day. And did they ever... I did not know this then, but that would be the last show we would ever play. Considering how much time and money we had invested in that album, it was somewhat absurd, and we may have rushed it slightly. We never got the opportunity to play the album's songs live.

This was because the drummer said he wanted to finish with the band as he would get married soon and could no longer have time for the band. The song "There's Just Now" on the album was written to get the drummer to stay in the band, but to no avail. We finished the album together and made some CDs to sell, but again, we just gave them away, and the band ended. The saddest part is that we never got to play these songs live on the new album.

When the band was no more, Greg was working on his next project, which was buying a house and redoing it into a nicer house, which was easier said than done. This place was a bit of a fixer-upper. It was in a suburb of Baltimore City called Arbutus. Greg's parents, especially his dad, were incredibly handy and could fix and work on all parts of the house to make it beautiful again, which he did with some help from the band friends. Our first job on Greg's new house was to gut the upstairs walls while Greg's parents, his dad, and stepdad were redoing the main floor floors, which went on to look beyond beautiful.

Once I met Abby at that show, I spent time with her and started to like her. We hung out and talked. One night, when we were putting on the insulation on the upstairs walls, Abby came over to drink just Greg, Abby, and me. We finished our work for the night and started to like each other a lot. We were very excited to drink together. It was even crazier for her to come to see me because it was around a 1-2 hour drive each way since she lived in the Philadelphia area. I was in Baltimore, Maryland. I was very excited to see her, and when the drinks started flowing, I started having a great time with Greg and Abby. The alcohol helped, but we were feeling each other a lot while kissing and stuff on the stairs. It was before Greg had any furniture, so we got intimate on the staircase. I think we both enjoyed ourselves. Since she lived so far away, we decided not to start a relationship, but we became friends from a distance.

After Abby, I took a little break from girls until Cinamonthia's birthday, when she and I started hanging out behind Chris's back while he liked her. I remember going to dinner for her birthday dinner, which was somewhat romantic and paid for by her older sister. She invited me, of all people, to her birthday dinner, just her and me. While living with Flutie in Baltimore, I started falling for her. The same girl from earlier in the story. This was a problem because Flutie was madly in love with her and would do anything for her. Since I was very attracted to her, too I made the depraved mistake of starting to hang out with her without telling Flutie. It was a very sneaky and not a great best friend move; my selfish desire took control.

We had always been great friends since high school. During this time, she was starting the police academy and pursuing her dream job as a police officer in Baltimore City. A few months before she started at the academy, I began to have feelings for her, and I decided to make her a Valentine's Day song with a small studio set up in my recording studio on my computer. This song is also on YouTube under my name, Cody W. Ridenour. I named this song "Cassia" to not upset Flutie, as the song was intended for Cinamonthia as her Valentine's Day gift. I did like her a lot, but I knew that I was in the wrong. During a giant snowstorm in early spring or late winter, I remember helping her shovel out her car early in the morning to get her to the academy on time and assisting her with breakfast and her morning routine. This relationship was short-lived, as I knew I was selfishly betraying one of my best friends—a genuinely great person. To this day, this is by far and unequivocally the worst thing I have ever done to a friend. Gosh, did he hate me during this time, and rightly so. I would have been upset with me too. Interestingly, when I was in middle school, she arrived one day as a new student, and I immediately made it my mission to meet and befriend her with beautiful cinnamon-colored skin which I did. Eventually, I invited her to my house to get in the hot tub, which we did. We talked a lot and ended up making out. It was my second-ever kiss. I liked her a lot, and quickly she became one of my lifelong friends. Even though it was not long after our hot tub night, she went to another guy's hot tub and did the same thing. I didn't fault her for it; I know it's never easy starting at a new school. So, I'm saying that she and I had some history before Flutie even met her. Not that this mattered. As a result of this situation, my friends and I started calling her HTH in middle school, which stood for hot tub hopper—sorry, Cinammonthia. Still, she and I became lifelong friends.

7

Facing
Danger

At this point, I was still splitting time between my parents and Flutie, despite my awful decision to betray one of my best friends by spending time with Cinammonthia. This action hurt our friendship fundamentally. Eventually, I decided to move into Greg's new house that he bought once he got a couch for me to sleep on in the TV room. Greg had been working at a successful heating and cooling company for years, and he quickly got me a job doing paperwork for the jobs the servicemen had previously done. It was a nice job, and I got paid much more than my previous job. I went to a better job with higher pay. This was my first-ever desk job, sitting in a chair all day. Honestly, it wasn't that bad; I could quietly listen to music throughout the day, and I would complete one hundred push-ups in a row during each lunch break while eating my childhood favorite peanut butter and jelly sandwich.

Now that Greg and I were living in his new house together and working on the house every weekend even more. During all these times in my life when Brady was gone in California, I was always very proud and jealous of him, even though it was difficult at times for him to stay afloat. Our family was always there for him, Mitch mostly, and if not Mitch, me. I may have shared some money with him during his most dire times. Brady is a fighter and lived in his car for a few months, but he did what he had to do to survive. I would do it again for him if needed because I have always believed in that man. He would do the same for me if I needed the money. That's love.

I worked for this cooling and heating company with Greg for around two months, since I had some money saved, I decided to visit Brady in California. At this point, Brady lived with a friend in the Navy who had a lovely house. I took a week off work to fly to San Diego to visit Brady and see what Southern California is all about. Greg graciously dropped me off at the airport. I would visit my best friend; in six short hours, I would see Brady for the first time since he moved to California.

I flew from Baltimore to Colorado on my way to San Diego, and I am glad I did. When I got on the plane from Colorado to San Diego, I couldn't help but notice a cute girl on the plane with me. I made it a point to talk to her when we exited the plane. The first thing I did upon landing was track down that pretty girl, and I did. I introduced myself and told her what I was doing in San Diego. She flew in from Colorado to visit her mother, who lived in southern California. We exchanged phone numbers, and I told her I was considering moving to San Diego if this visit went well. We planned to get together during my trip. Her name is Cheyenne.

The first thing Brady had me do on this visit was go rock climbing, very high up, and I was terrified. It was a rite of passage for Brady and his friends. I did not love it, but I had to push through. I never had any problems with heights before, but this was different for some reason; it was terrifying this time. We then proceeded to a nearby burrito establishment and holy smokes; it was phenomenal.

The highlights of the trip to visit Brady in San Diego were as follows: rock climbing, drinking a little at a few different bars, going to get some awesome burritos, exploring the wealthy parts of La Jolla, seeing the seals, and just exploring and spending time with Brady and then getting close to Cheyenne and meeting Brady's hilarious roommate, Chad. Next, Brady showed me a spot with a nice nude beach with a cliff going down to it with a path. I had such a great time on the trip. Upon returning to Maryland, I worked a little longer to save money and decided to move to San Diego to live with Brady in a few months.

As I was planning my move to California, unbeknownst to me, my parents were working on their own move. Mitch's parents had a very awesome and beautiful beach house in the Ocean City, MD, area that both of my parents loved. They admired the beach it was close to, and the surrounding area and it would be a great place for Shane to experience as he was growing up. The fact that Mitch's parents had this house was huge for our family and the future, especially since Mitch was not able to make the money that he once did now that he was on disability with heart failure. Making the payments for the house in Hampstead was becoming more complex. The opportunity to take over this home was great! Especially since this beach house was paid for. All my brothers were out of the house except for my youngest brother, Shane. Devin was a freshman in college. Brady was in San Diego with my plan of moving to live with him after the drive with Eric, my lead guitarist to try our luck with music out there. My dear parents were excited for sure, and they had even started a plan for building a fence for the dogs. Things were looking up for the next adventure for the family. The book was on the table at this moment so much that Mitch's parents canceled the buyer they had set up to sell the house to and decided that they were going to sell it to Mitch instead. The problems in the world were finally getting smaller for the family.

I was incredibly excited to move, especially because I would move with Eric Holderman, who had quickly become my favorite person to write and record music with and one of my best friends. We had the dream of creating a band in San Diego together. I got everything together, said goodbye to my friends and family, and we were almost ready to go. Eric and I decided to record one last song. We decided to call this song "All the Miles." You should also find this song on YouTube, Cody W. Ridenour, under my name. In this song, Eric Holderman played the lead guitar and the drums. He is a man of many talents. Eric and I packed everything into our separate cars and went on an incredible adventure! Before I left, Flutie and I were still not on great terms, but he wished us luck.

It was the heat of summer, and we decided to take the northern route. The first state we crossed into was Ohio. This will go down in history as my least favorite state in America because after driving for just a few hours, I got my first and only ticket on the trip for speeding. I think it was Eric Holderman's idea because it became illegal to talk on the phone while driving not long before our trip. We bought walkie-talkies to communicate without using our phones. We were very excited about sightseeing in these beautiful places we had never been to before. I had received advice on places to stop on our way from my airplane buddy, Cheyanne. We followed most of the drive. Our first stop was in Cleveland, Ohio, to see the Rock and Roll Hall of Fame. We arrived, walked in, and realized you must pay to enter. Since we were both trying to save as much money as possible, we decided to get food instead of going in, which was also cool. It was funny; after walking around the city for about 20 minutes, we realized it was the cleanest city we had ever been to. We thought it felt like we were on a TV set because no one was walking around in the city. It was empty to us. Then, it was back on the road again. We drove for a few hours; I don't know how long, but it was nighttime when we got to our next stop.

This was Chicago, Illinois. It was very nice, but we didn't explore a ton. We saw and felt the crazy wind, a strange above-ground subway, and the Sears Tower. It was pretty huge. We saw a restaurant with a hilarious name; it was called Poag Mahone's. It was going to be Eric's new alter ego, Poag Mahone. Our next stop was somewhere in Nebraska, near Omaha, where we stopped to eat dinner. We also took an incredible picture of the sunset before dinner time. We also made a friend that Eric met before we continued our journey. I'm sure you're curious about where we stopped to sleep. Well, we slept in our cars in Walmart parking lots every night. It was free, and they had nice bathrooms. We continued to I think, Iowa. It was a very relaxing place, right by the river, with a beautiful bridge overlooking it. We talked to a local and then we drove to Idaho. I thought it was cool because it was a different landscape than we had just come from, with some very crazy rocks and kind of a desert feel. The town Cheyanne sent us reminded me of an old western town, minus one minor detail. In this town there was a law that if you wanted to buy any alcohol, you had to buy a food item too. We bought the cheapest thing on the menu, which was French fries. Cheyanne sent us here because there was an incredible state park with a massive rock monolith. Like everything else in America, it wasn't free, so we did not explore it.

Onto our next stop, Utah. The most exciting thing on our drive through Utah was that we stopped to shower at a truck stop after a few days of driving and sleeping in our cars since we did not smell great. We paid a small amount and got to shower at the truck stop, and then we were back on the road. We went on our way. Our next stop was Nevada to see the Grand Canyon. This could be our only chance ever to see it. We were both exhausted from driving all day when we got to Nevada. We stopped in for the night in a small parking lot. The whole time we were sleeping in this deserted town, there were cops in trucks watching us sleep all night. Was it because this was a completely deserted town? The first and last I ever encountered. To this day, Eric and I have no idea why. We drove on and headed to the road that led us to the Grand Canyon. This was a part of the trip I was most looking forward to seeing, and I was not disappointed! It was everything I could have dreamed of and more. I felt I had no choice but to take a few incredibly dangerous pictures from crazy high up, where if I had fallen, I indeed would have died. Eric kept telling me to stop until I finally did. Then Eric and I quickly put the pictures on Facebook. My parents were not super happy I was doing that, but I had outstanding balance and was athletic. I knew I would be fine. Which I was. If you look up my Facebook, you can see those dangerous pictures of us at the Grand Canyon. Eric kept telling me I was doing too many dangerous things there. I felt in control the whole time. I trusted my body, and I had good control of my body and legs because of my playing sports and training my body and legs my whole life.

Once Eric and I finished our view of the Grand Canyon, we returned to our next stop, Colorado, where Cheyanne's mom lived. The first thing we noticed when we got into Colorado was the number of snow-capped mountains in the heat of summer. It blew my mind. Seeing and feeling how much the temperature changed on our drive was alarming. It started at around 80 degrees and went down to about 50 in a matter of hours. As we drove up and up, the craziest thing to me was that while we were driving through the mountains, some of the peaks were so high that my car struggled to drive up them. Our cars were fighting hard on the road between the wind and the mountain peaks. After much more driving, we ended up in Cheyanne's mom's town in Colorado. The first thing we did was buy some completely legal marijuana at a dispensary—the first one we had been to. It was cool because it was the first time we could buy it legally. While Cheyanne was working, we explored a little and Eric found a room where there was an incredible and beautiful piano that he was playing. I think it was at Colorado State University. I finally got to see Cheyanne again, and we stayed at her apartment for a night. It was nice because we got to sleep on something much more comfortable than the front seats of our cars. I was lucky to sleep in a comfy bed with a pretty girl. I remember that we all went hiking in the morning. I had such a awesome time with the mountains close by and the very different kind of nature. I have always loved hiking, especially in new places. I think my fondest memory of visiting her was our hiking adventure. Then, it was right back on the road for the last leg of our trip to live in California. To me, and I'm sure to Eric, this was by far the coolest part of the trip. Not only because we were getting closer to being in California finally but because this was the first time either of us had ever seen a real desert in person, and it blew our freaking minds. Eric decided this spot would be his thinking spot in our new home. As we drove to a secluded part of California, the excitement grew every mile, with the growing desert dunes and barren, devoid-of-life landscape. I grew to appreciate it more and more as we continued. In the rolling hills and dunes of the desert I will never forget.

As we crept into civilization again, we arrived at our new home. The first thing we did upon arriving at Brady's friend's place was take a quick nap. Then Brady took us to an excellent local bar with so many different beers to choose from. The first local girl I met in California was a bartender who must've been having a bad day because she was not very nice to me, but Brady says she is usually very nice. It happens sometimes to everyone. I saved a lot of money to start my new life, so I had a small cushion of cash available to me for a time before I had to start looking for work. I used this time to share experiences with Brady and Eric.

The first few days were spent exploring the area and resting a little. One of the first days I can remember in our new lives in San Diego maybe day four or five, I had to go pick Brady up because he was stranded somewhere out and about on his motorcycle. Being the great brother that I am, I drove Chad's nice Jeep to pick him up and rescue him from the rare heavy rain.

It was cool because I got the chance to drive Chad's nice Jeep. Chad is the nicest dude. He had just separated from his wife, which was difficult for him. We all loved that guy, and he owned the house. The next night, we went to the bar together and enjoyed playing pool. Brady has always been great at it. I introduced myself to the prettiest girl at the bar. Her name is Kristy, and wouldn't you know it, it was her birthday, and she was there celebrating with her friends. I'm not sure what I said to get her to like me, but she and I are still friends. I recall sharing a brief but pleasant moment of affectionate kissing before we departed from the bar. It was satisfying for both of us. It was a nice little birthday gift for us both.

The next day, I spent applying to jobs, trying to be productive after a quick run. I spent the rest of the night partying with Eric, Chad, and Brady, with some playing guitar thrown in the mix. Later that night, I decided that I was going to smoke the most cannabis I ever had in my life at this point. Why not? I was already productive that day, applying to jobs, running and playing guitar. I deserved it? at least it was legal.

The next morning, Eric and Chad were hungover, and I had energy because I only smoked a ton of weed. So, no hangover for this guy. While my roommates were resting and Brady was on a job interview, I decided that I was going to take this early afternoon or late morning to enjoy the southern California nature by going on a hike. I told

Chad and Eric I would return in a few hours. I chose the Ho Chi Minh Trail in La Jolla. Little did I know, this is one of the more challenging trails in the area. A huge, detailed sign warned that you should only use this hike if you are an experienced hiker. I was very athletic and very confident in my body. I went on my way hiking. The California sky was cloudless, the breeze was gentle, and the temps were in the low 80s. Only the hawks circling overhead gave a warning: creatures lacking wings were better off on the ground.

I passed a sketchy-looking bridge I had to hike past to continue the trail. Of course, I had to take a picture of it to send to Shane and Brady via Snapchat with the caption, "Sketchy, just the way I like it." This would be the last memory I would ever have of June 8th, 2016. After around four hours. Eventually, Brady finished his interview, returned home, and went to the bathroom quickly.

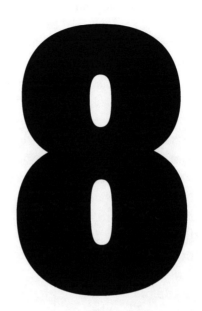

8

A Phone
Call

When I was going to a job interview, Cody texted me, asking if I wanted to go on a hike. I said I couldn't until later since I had a job interview. I was returning to Chad's house from a job interview and received a Snapchat from Cody showing a little log bridge. I replied, "hell yeah," but I never got a response. When I got back to Chad's, Eric and Chad were there. I put my phone down on the counter and started talking to everyone. Eric (I think) said, "Brady, your phone is ringing." It was a number I didn't know but a California number. I picked up and said, "Hello." The voice on the other side said, "Hi, is this Brady?" I said, "Yeah," and the person on the phone said, "This is Lieutenant Something" (I can't remember his name, maybe Dan), "with the San Diego lifeguard, I'm calling about Cody." (I had thought they were calling about a job you applied for since you put me down as a reference for the jobs.) I said, "Yeah, that's my brother." That's when he said, "Your brother was involved in a hiking accident, and it's not looking good. We flew him to Scripps La Jolla, but it looks bad." Then the lieutenant started to hint that if I needed anyone to talk to, he could set me up with them (assuming he wouldn't make it). I knew it was bad when he said, "It's not looking good." His voice was very somber, and it was difficult for him to tell me what he was telling me.

He then gave me the number and the name of the contact at the hospital. I didn't have a car then, looked Chad dead in the face, and said, "I need your car right now; where are your keys?" Eric was just about frozen in place while Chad handed me his keys as he continued to ask, "Who was that on the phone? Is everything alright? What's going on?" Knowing nothing but confusion and concern. He handed me his keys in the kitchen and asked as I walked out, "Is everything okay?" One last time. I replied while walking out the door, trying to stay calm. "I don't know, dude. I don't know." He started to ask more questions, but I just dipped. I didn't want to explain anything to them until I knew what was happening. I didn't want to deal with two more distressed and confused people.

I remember going down the highway, and one side of me was saying to go as fast as the car would let me go, and the other side of me was saying to make sure you drive so you make it to the hospital. So, I split the difference. Fast enough that if I did get pulled over, I wouldn't be going to jail, so I would still make it to the hospital. I can't remember if I called the hospital or if they called me, but we started talking. I remember having to identify you to the doctors because you didn't have any identification. A lady at the desk in the hospital proceeded to ask me questions like what color his hair was, how tall he was, and something like what Cody was wearing. I hadn't seen him, so I had to remember what shoes he had. I confirmed his identity. I got to the hospital and parked. I walked in and they had a bunch of people (60–80 years of age). I couldn't tell if it was a volunteer group or hospital patients singing songs in this side section of the lobby. I went to the front desk and had to talk to the lady at the desk and figure out how to get to Cody. Someone that I spoke to ended up telling me to go to the emergency room to sign a s*** load of papers.

I then went to the surgery waiting room. I ran into the doctor he said, "Oh, are you Brady?" I said, "Yeah!" He said, "We just finished the first surgery; everything looks good; however, he is in rough shape." Not even 5 minutes later, I saw him running down the hallway in an obvious, alarming panic. He saw me and stopped for the briefest second and wildly explained, "We are rushing Cody back to surgery; he started bleeding in the brain again; this is not good." Then he rushed off. I went up to this big TV that had the surgeries on a schedule and the amount of time.

So, I sat there and kept my eye on it. When I fully grasped the severity of the situation, I knew I had to call Mom and Mitch. I was terrified to have to explain to them what was going on.

I went to the entrance, walked in, and leaned against a parking ticket kiosk. I opened my phone and called Mitch since I knew I couldn't break that news to mom. I can't remember if he picked up the first time or what, but I began to tell him the best I could. The conversation went like this: Mitch picked up, and I said, "Hey," and before I could get another word out, he said, "What's wrong?" I replied with a couple ums and finally got it out. "Cody's been in an accident, and he's at the hospital." Mitch asked, "S***, Jesus Christ, how bad is it?" I said, "It's really bad." His next question was, "Is he going to make it?" I replied, "I don't know." I'm pretty sure Mitch then said, "Bridge, Bridge, come here." This is the only time I remember hearing Mitch lose his cool and break down. He said, "Call my parents right now and have them watch the kids right now. We got to go." Mom remained pretty calm, aside from the initial Jesus Christ. Mitch said, "I'm buying plane tickets right now. I'll see you in the morning. Just hang tight." We said I love you and got off the phone. I called Chad and filled him in on the situation. I remember people walking into the hospital and looking over at me as I was having this conversation. Chad freaked a little, then was like damn dude, he was coming right now. What do you need? "Are you hungry, thirsty, dude, anything?" I was like maybe some drinks and snacks; at this point, we all knew we would be there for a long time. Then Corey Huber, one of my great friends, called me. He was so concerned that I caught him up to speed. We talked a little longer and a couple more times that night. I was receiving one call after another while figuring everything out. I walked back in, and next to the surgery room was a quiet room. It was like a small room with no windows, maybe eight chairs, and some coffee tables with lamps and boxes of tissues on them. They also had a whole lot of prayer and comfort books. That's when the weight of the situation hit me. Damn, I'm in the quiet room; this is "f***ing gnarly." It gave me time to stay silent and unbothered. I remember I walked in feeling like it was a 50/50 shot that he would make it. It truly could go either way. This was such an unknown. I sat down and vividly remembered this thought: "My kids and my family might never know Uncle Cody, my brother." He could live on as a memory. A story about him that I tell them about: this wasn't easy to face, and there's a chance that could be the case at any moment that day.

Chad then showed up with six bags of gas station snacks and drinks. We hung out in the waiting room for quite a while. It seemed like 10 hours before someone came in to let us know that the surgeries were done and Cody was being taken to a room in the ICU. The nurse said someone would come to get us when Cody was all set up in the room. We're thinking, cool; we'll get to see you soon. We sat down there for another 2–3 hours before someone came to bring us up. The nurse reminded us that Cody looked bad as we were being taken up. We went in, and indeed, he looked in really bad shape. (We later found out it took so long because they wanted to replace Cody's bandages so he didn't look as bad.) Everyone explained that the next 24 hours were critical. The one major rule was to be quiet. Like, make no noise at all. So, all three of us—Chad, Eric, and I—sat there and waited for Mitch and Mom to arrive. Eventually, my parents arrived, and they got the full scoop. When the time was right, Brady posted a Facebook post that said, "pray for my brother." Once that post was published, the messages and phone calls started pouring in. One phone call that I thought was beautiful was a call from Zauhn, in which I explained the situation, and we both agreed that if anyone could get through this okay, it was Cody. He always had this very strong willpower; if he had an idea to do something, he would get it done no matter what it took.

9

Doctor
Nasarallah

In preparation for this part of the book, I contacted one of the doctors who worked on me at Scripps Memorial Hospital in La Jolla, California, one of the best-ranked trauma hospitals in the country. I was lucky that I was so close. If this dire situation had to happen, I'm very grateful that it transpired so close to this hospital.

This doctor's name is Dr. Nasrallah. Multiple doctors, technicians, and nurses worked on my case, saving my life. Unfortunately, I only had the opportunity to talk with Dr. Nasrallah. It was a good thing, too. Dr. Fady was a great help with every possible question I had about my case. Again, thank you for your help with closing in the gaps during my comatose time and for all the information I now have from the doctors who pulled together to give me a second chance at life.

I came into the hospital in a coma because of the incredible amount of pain; the doctors induced me to make sure I stayed in and didn't wake up. The first thing he said was that I sustained three different kinds of bleeding on both sides of the brain. This needed immediate surgery to relieve the pressure in the brain by evacuating the blood on one side. Then, after the surgery, the other side of the brain swelled, requiring the skull to be removed completely until the swelling improved. It was replaced about six weeks later and kept in a cooler until then. There were skull fractures on both sides of the skull that needed repair. CFS (a type of liquid that surrounds the brain and spinal cord and cushions the brain and spinal cord from injury while also delivering nutrition and removing waste) leaked through the ears from the fracture. The skull was shattered and pieced backed together. I have an x-ray of my new skull and it is crazy (On the back cover). There was a blood clot in one of the veins in the brain (the sagittal sinus). If it got to a part of the brain and couldn't pass through it, it could have caused more brain damage. I was put on blood thinners until the clot was resolved. I had multiple facial fractures that didn't require surgery. It is crazy, but I broke almost every bone in the face, including both eye sockets and my nose, though not a single tooth. I even broke the roof of my mouth. Thank God again because Mitch would have killed me if I had broken any teeth. He spent a lot of money to fix my crooked teeth. In fact, my braces fixed my jaw too. I suffered bruises and a tear in one lung as a result of breaking 11 of my 12 ribs (interestingly, one rib received no damage at all). This required a tube in the chest wall to evacuate the leaking air in the chest and allow the lung to heal the tear while sticking to the chest wall. This was essential for my lungs to heal, with two collapsed lungs. If they didn't heal correctly, the lungs could have been permanently damaged. Luckily, they recovered. I had respiratory failure, requiring me to be on a ventilator for several weeks, including a tracheostomy (a tube directly into my windpipe through the bottom of my neck). Eventually, as I became more coherent, I ripped the trachea out (this was when I was out of the ICU, and it was only once).

There was a kidney laceration, which needed no intervention (surgery) since it was not severe enough to cause a urine leak. Fun fact: humans can live with only half of a kidney. My right hip was dislocated. This required a procedure done in the trauma bay to put it back into place. My left forearm bone was fractured (the bigger one). This one needed surgery to stabilize it and maintain my hand and wrist function. This was done by putting in some metal parts for a while to help heal. Lumbar transverse fractures (the spikes on the sides of the vertebrae in the lower back) heal without surgery. I was also informed that I came out of the coma with partial paralysis on my left side. My mom told me that after my brain surgeries, I contracted a life-threatening fever. I know that over 107 Fahrenheit can cause death. I'm not sure what the exact temperature was, but my mom remembers that the doctors had to completely cover my whole body with ice to get it to go down. This is a common experience for a patient during a brain injury called neurostorming, in which the sympathetic nervous system (SNS), responsible for the flight response, becomes confused after a severe brain injury. This causes a fever. The doctor also told me that my temperature spiked once again when my skull was put back on. Not nearly as high. The last thing the doctor wrote for me was this: "All in all, you sustained a fall of 50-60 feet down off a cliff. Mortality is approximately 50%. I would call that a win!

Use that to win to do something good." He told me that I came into the ER after being airlifted into the hospital. I must have fallen and rolled into a little crevasse as I fell. Luckily, a couple who saw the whole thing were hiking behind me and contacted the closest lifeguard in the area. This lifeguard, "Rick," eventually sent me pictures of me getting airlifted, where I was found, and an idea of what could have happened. He called 911, found me, and got me to the hospital (which was very lucky again, only miles away). The doctors and hospital workers worked on me when I arrived at the ER. They had their work cut out for them. There is still a YouTube video of the San Diego news of my lifeless body being airlifted via helicopter. Here is the link to the video: https://youtu.be/hoZkoSfM2WU. You will also see some pictures of the place where I fell, taken by the lifeguard with whom I was found, a helpful lifesaver. I cannot thank everyone enough for helping. I hope to thank him in person one day. Maybe the craziest thing about this whole thing is that if I hadn't fallen on my head and broken my skull immediately I almost surely would have died. The fact that I broke my skull into pieces saved my life. It gave my brain a little room. Lucky break, literally.

One thing I forgot to mention when I was in the hospital: I had a lot of trouble with catheters, repeatedly experiencing urinary tract infections over the months. It must've caused a great deal of pain. As I was finally becoming more coherent, Brady remembered that I would punch myself in the bladder often. He also recalls how much it hurt him to watch me go through all this agony while the doctors re-installed my skull. I was in a twilight state of animation while my temperature went up again.

There was nothing to do but watch and pray. I can scarcely imagine what it was like to see me go through this as a brother, not to mention as a mother who never once left my side. I apologize profusely for putting you all through this. It was an extenuating circumstance. If I have shown you all (my family) anything, it's that no matter the situation, I will not give up. I fervently hope that this vital aspect of my personality gave you some comfort as I fought for my life.

From the moment that my mom arrived at the hospital in California, she never left until I did. As most people imagine this situation was challenging for her, mainly because we were always close. As you can remember, John was not a fan from the moment I was born with my red hair. My mom always loved me unconditionally, as all parents should love their kids. The way that Mitch always did, no matter how difficult I made it. I always tell people that John helped create me, but Mitch is entirely my dad. When John heard about the situation, he did nothing except ask Brady if he should come to see me. Thankfully, Brady said no. He said he wanted to help financially, but John couldn't because he was putting on a new roof on his house at the time.

When my mom got word of the danger I was in, she

immediately came to my aid, catching the first flight with no time to waste. I'm sure you can imagine how difficult it is for her to talk about those days, even after all these years. I think it was just as traumatic for her as it was for me, maybe even more. I will do my best to try to get some information from her perspective, but I am not promising anything.

When Mitch heard the news, he immediately got a plane ticket for my mom, and she was off. I think the worst thing was that my mom had no idea what to expect when arriving at the hospital after the 6-hour flight. Brady only told them that I was in surgery. That's as much as he knew. I mean, what the heck could have been going on in her mind during this long flight.

10

I'm Sorry
Mom

After hearing about Cody's accident from Brady, Mitch immediately called the hospital. They confirmed the tragic news. Cody had fallen off a cliff and suffered severe head trauma; they said that he might not make it through the night. I took the first flight to San Diego. During the flight, I tried not to think about anything and just cleared my mind.

When I got to the hospital and saw you for the first time, it was immediately apparent that the situation was far worse than I imagined. Your head was bandaged, your eyes were black, and you had tubes in your nose, mouth, and throat. You were also on a ventilator, and there was dried blood in your ears. You also had tubes that were draining blood from your abdomen. The doctor explained how important the next three days would be. This is how long it takes for the brain to reach its peak swelling before it starts to recede. They removed the skull to allow this to happen. If you hadn't cracked your skull when you fell, the blood would have been trapped, and you would have died at the scene. When the brain swelling reached its peak, it was shocking. Your face swelled up so badly that you were unrecognizable. It was hard to look at you. I don't ever want to look at something like that again. After three days, as the swelling was slowly going down, chances got a little better that you might live. Not a lot, but you had reached the first of many milestones. However, due to the seriousness of the brain injury, no one could predict the progress you would make, if any. One doctor used the word 'horrendous' to describe the extent of the trauma that your brain had sustained. It was my first time hearing a doctor use that word, especially to the parents. It seemed there was little hope that you would have anything even close to a normal life. Every day a doctor would tell us, 'This might be all you ever get.' At this point, we didn't know what that meant—

whether you had to be on a ventilator all your life or not. However, the doctor would also tell us that you had youth on your side and not to lose all hope. We liked that. The doctors never candy-coated anything or gave us false hopes and I respected their honesty.

I wondered how many women would cry so much in this situation, but not me. My whole life, I've prepared for the worst and hoped for the best. If you can accept and deal with the worst-case scenario, everything else is a gift. I am the most emotional person ever, but in severe situations I am calm. I always protect everyone else and cry later. I go into this mode where my emotions shut off and are put on hold. I don't cry. I can accomplish that; I would be in this protection mode, but I would weep in tears if a vehicle honked at me in traffic. It is an instinct.

You had staples on both sides of your head from your forehead back in a "V" shape. Even after the swelling in your brain receded, they waited until the area became overly concave like a spoon before they put the skull back on. We were always so afraid of touching that area. Not only was it soft, but I thought that if I did, my finger would go through the skin and I'd be touching your brain. The doctor finally explained that the brain has a strong membrane protecting it, much like the soft spots on a baby's head. I felt better, but I still wouldn't touch it.

Eventually, the ventilator helped your collapsed lungs and the punctured lung healed enough for you to breathe on your own, marking another milestone safely. A couple of weeks later, you went through something extremely worrisome. You developed a high fever and they couldn't bring it down. Many people were in your room, placing ice packs almost everywhere on your body. The monitor registered in Celsius, not Fahrenheit, and I remember it being in the 40s. They finally covered you in a special thick blanket attached to a machine that pumped ice water through it. I was told that high fevers are typical for a severe brain injury, as the brain is learning to regulate temperature again. When the fever subsided you made it through another milestone.

After a couple more weeks, you started opening your eyes. It was barely halfway, and not for long. The more conscious you became, the harder it was for you to tolerate. First, you started moaning with extremely painful facial expressions. Then, your legs began moving uncontrollably. You would constantly slide your heels, one at a time, up and down along the bed whenever you were awake. Your moaning became louder and never stopped when you were awake. It was so loud that everyone on the 5th floor could hear you. Your leg movements would cause your whole body to move sideways across the bed until your legs were hanging off one side and your head was against the side rail. I was constantly calling the nurses to reposition you back on the bed. You couldn't be left alone.

I remember this one time when a nurse came to check your vitals between moans, and as clear as day, you said," Get me the f*** out of here." I looked at the nurse, and she looked at me, and I said, "Did you... and she said, "Yep." This was the first and only thing you ever said. If the nurse hadn't witnessed it, I would have thought I was crazy and hearing things. Plus, you never used to cuss! After that, you had to learn to talk much later along the line. Brady visited every day and I always looked forward to it. It was unbearable to listen to you moan in agony all day. He would sneak me in some Not Your Father's Root Beer. The bottles looked like root beer instead of alcohol, and I drank from Styrofoam cups. It kept me sane. We kept each other sane. One day, we talked about how, when you get better, you will form another band. We even came up with your next CD:

> Band: Comatose
> Album: Scripps 504
> Featuring the hits, "Falling for You, "Head Over
Heels, and "Rock Bottom
> Other Songs included are: "Bone Flap Fantasies."
> "The sponge Bath Shuffle"
> "ICU Later"
> "Trachea it Outta Me"
> "The Catheter Blues"
> "Staple Head"
> "Rehab Me at Hello"
> "The Red Head Rock"

I remember the first obstacle we had to overcome. The hospital asked for your insurance card a few days after you arrived. We told them it was in your wallet. They said they were with your personal belongings. The hospital policy said they could not release them to anyone except a spouse. When they were told that you're not married, they still refused. Your keys were also with the belongings, and we had to find your car and move it before it was towed. It was found. Fanny, a social worker in the hospital, helped work it out. It took a couple of days but Mitch got it done. Little did he know it was only the start of all the bureaucratic challenges he would have to deal with throughout your recovery. Fast forward to when your insurance company decided there was nothing more the hospital could do for your recovery. We had to find somewhere else for you to go after the hospital. Mitch was in a race to find a nursing home that would accept you before the insurance company stopped paying for the hospital stay. Not only did you have a feeding tube, but you still had no control over your movements. For this reason, you would occasionally get a finger caught in a wire and pull it out. They had to put a pillow on your hands, resembling boxing gloves. When a patient must wear boxing gloves, they are considered combative, and no one would accept them. You were still barely conscious at this time. For the gloves to come off, I had to stay up all night to watch you. If nothing got pulled out in 24 hours, the hospital could remove your gloves, and you would no longer be considered combative. We finally found a nursing home that, because of your age, decided to take you on as a patient. It was close to home in Maryland. The problem was how to get you home. You were 3000 miles away! You couldn't control your movements, and you had to be strapped onto a stretcher for travel. You also still had a feeding tube and a couple of IVs. Our only choice to get you home was an air ambulance. The insurance company would not help pay for it. The fight home was in a small Learjet with two paramedics, costing us $28,000 out of pocket. Many people helped us through GoFundMe.

It turned out that this nursing home was the place you were meant to be. They even made an exception for one of us to stay overnight in your room, something they've never done. You were still moving your legs uncontrollably and ending up sideways in bed, almost falling off. I'm sure they were relieved that someone was there to keep an eye on you. Little did I know you would be blessed with the best rehabilitation staff one could ask for.

Mitch had a high school friend who lived in California. He passed away, but Mitch stayed in contact with his wife. She lived 20 minutes away from the hospital. She came to visit, and she brought me a bag with magazines. At the bottom, there was a bottle of wine. Gina was so nice. I hadn't met her in person before. The first time I saw her was in the hospital.

I would shower at Gina's house because I lived in

Cody's room. I tried to shower at her house at least once a week. I didn't want to bother Brady by asking him to stay with Cody, but I didn't want to leave his side. I was in mom mode. Also, because I didn't want him to suffer, I tried to keep him as close to me as possible. I appreciated the nurse who always would tell me, "You need to take a break. You need to leave; you need to go shower and rest." In the morning, I would wake up, wait for you to get calm and sleep, then go to the bathroom, brush my teeth, make a ponytail, and go to the coffee shop. Then, back to the room.

So many people were sending me things to Chad's house, where Brady was staying—stuff like deodorant, calming sprays, money, t-shirts, snacks, and games. People cared about me when I was there. I am so grateful for them. There was no night or morning for me. It could be four in the morning or five in the afternoon. You would be screaming, moaning, and just shaking your legs. You would bring your knees to your chest and back down, moaning. The whole floor would hear you. They had to put foam, pillows, and wrap around your ankles to prevent sores as you would slide your heels up and down on the bed all day and night. It was horrible the whole time. You had the pain in your face and a psychological torture moan. The moaning was pain. If you think screaming has to do with fear, this moaning was excruciating pain. I hope I will never hear that again. It f***s with your head. Moaning, and you feel so helpless. There is nothing that you can do. It was so terrible. Cody would never cry. I saw one tear one time. I was sitting next to him, trying to comfort him, and he looked at me with his mouth open, and one tear came down. Only one. I used to put my headphones on to block out the sound, but I couldn't block out the sight. I needed to be aware to keep him from falling. It did shake me up psychologically. I had to be there and be strong. As a mother, you can't get away from your son. Every time I went to smoke outside, I would look up to heaven, pray for strength, and tell God, I love you. Always saying, You got this. Like He always does.

I don't even remember that much because I had to be sane. I had to keep him safe, so he wouldn't fall off a bed and hit his head again. I barely slept. It was so hard to go through it and get the facts and memories straight; I refuse to go through that again. I fought so hard to stay sane. When you hear people go through a huge tragedy, they survive because they block out the bad memories. At that exact moment, I couldn't block it because I had to be there to protect him. What helped me was listening to the right songs. I also listened to Saosin's song "You're Not Alone" a lot. This song, "Atlas Falls" from Shinedown, is the one that came out after his accident, but every time I listen to it, I cannot think about other things. This one grabs my heart and puts me back in time. "Don't give up now." "I'll rise up and carry us all the way." That makes me remember Cody back there, even these days. There are songs that remind me of him. I'm sure the nurses were so grateful I was there because they had so much to do outside his room.

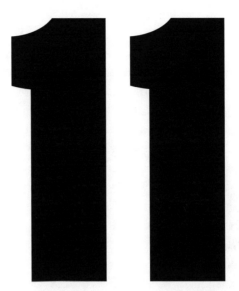

11

Proverbs
17:17

"A friend loves at all times and a brother is born for adversity." ESV

It was a weekday night, and I was chilling in Arizona in a hot tub, just looking at Facebook. I saw a post from Brady that said, "Pray for my brother." I immediately texted Bridget and said, "What happened to Cody?" After sending this text, I immediately called her directly. She went on to explain that he fell off a cliff and that he was currently in emergency surgery. She didn't know all the details; it was a mixed story. She proceeded to tell me about the hospital that he was at. She didn't know all the details herself. Bridget told me that she would fly to California that night. As I thought to myself, I thought Arizona is not far from San Diego. About five hours, but it looks close on a map. At this time in my life, I hated Cody. (You remember why). Upon hearing all this news, I thought about everything: our relationship and whatever else. Then I went to bed. I mean, before he destroyed our relationship by sleeping with the girl I was wildly infatuated with, we were attached at the hip as far as our friendship—the closest of friends.

The next day, I got up and went to work as usual. As my day started at the office, I could not shake the thought, "Holy s***, what if Cody is dying?"

I didn't know what was happening and realized I couldn't focus on anything at work. I thought, man, f*ck this; I have to go there. Before I did, I prayed on it. So, I started looking for plane tickets, which were far too expensive at the last minute. I thought, f˙ck! I'll get a bus. At 10 in the morning, I bought a bus ticket from Arizona to San Diego. I had nothing packed, just the clothes I was wearing, and that was it. I was at work and said, "Someone, please take me to the bus station." I got on the bus, which was a 15-hour bus ride. Driving through LA was awful. When I finally arrived, Eric Holderman picked me up from the bus station at 3 in the morning. Upon being picked up by Eric, we drove to the hospital. Cody had surgery the night before, "he was f*ck." When I arrived at the hospital, only Bridget was there because it was like 4 in the morning. I hung out with Cody for a little while, and that was when the severity of the situation came into view.

Then Eric Holderman and I went back to Chad's and smoked a ton of weed. We went to bed at seven in the morning. The next day came, and me and Eric woke up at about ten and waited for Brady to get up at around 12. Then we went back to the hospital again. That was the daily routine for the next week. I was visiting the hospital, wearing all Cody's clothes, and hanging out with Mitch. I was there for five days with no clothes, toothbrush, or anything, using all his stuff and sleeping on the couch until I took a bus back to Arizona. These were very stressful days for Mitch, as he had to figure everything out on the fly. It must have been challenging for him, but if anyone could do it, it was Mitch.

Every day was a little bit different, something new. Spending time with Cody, spending time with Mitch, and spending time with Bridget. On day 3, I had to find Cody's car. No one knew where he parked. So, Brady and I were driving around looking for his "f***ing" car and where it could be. Eventually, we did find it. We knew where he was hiking, so Brady thought deeply about where he could have parked to go hiking. We drove through many parking lots and eventually found his car in a residential neighborhood. It was just parked on the side of the street. It was like three or four hours of searching. Brady spotted it and yelled, "That's it right there!" After finally finding it, we drove it back to the house after this strenuous search.

Our daily routine was as follows: wake up, wait for Brady to wake up, go to the hospital for hours, get food with

Cody's parents, and learn about brain stuff with Mitch. All while Eric was fully unraveling. I'm not sure exactly why Eric could not deal with the situation. It was such a difficult situation for Eric that I spent much of my time talking to him. I got this same information from multiple sources. When Cody fell off the cliff, Eric kind of lost his mind, talking about suicide and all sorts of crazy stuff.

Eric did not deal with the accident well at all. It was very difficult for everyone involved. This was a very difficult situation, especially for me. I had to call out of work multiple times, and I felt bad that I eventually had to go home and leave his parents to deal with the absurdity of this situation on their own. I knew they would be okay but, the more help they could get the better. One night, I remember I went to a bar with Brady, who was struggling. It's crazy to think about it now, but we went to the bar and then got drunk and went right back to the hospital. At least we got some kind of remedy through this troubling time. I distinctly remember watching the tubes go out of his chest and his head every time we would go to see him in the room. All of that stuck with me. The tubes would pour out into a bucket as we sat with him. Other memories that stuck with me were all his conversations with Mitch during these five days, learning about his younger days, where he came from, and his crazy Jewish mafia family ties.

(One thing my whole family learned throughout this entire process was the kind of man that Flutie is. The kind of friend he is. He was one of my favorite people even before he showed his true colors, which are great colors. As you can see, Flutie is a genuinely beautiful person and an unquestionably faithful friend. I love this man back to the story.) I would watch as tubes drained into a clear bucket, and I would watch as they filled up with drainage fluid. It was gross to see and crazy to watch as my best friend continued to drain fluid from his brain and chest. Another crazy thing that I told him was that I would get phone calls from people who wanted to talk to him throughout the day. The only person he let speak to him was Cinamonthia. This was very difficult for me. I still very much loved her.

It was hard for me because I didn't realize or understand their relationship, and he would later assure him that it was not serious. We were merely good friends who got together once, with no feelings attached. Rachel, another girl we knew from high school, once visited Cody at the hospital once. She just happened to be in San Diego when he was in the hospital after the accident. She was always very friendly and pretty, but we thought she was out of our league in school. We were always friends in high school. I guess that's why she came to visit. It was incredibly thoughtful of her to come. Since no one knew at this point if Cody would die or not and if he did live, what kind of life would he have. She texted me, and said she was in the area and wanted to see if she could come and see me at the hospital. He asked Mitch and Mitch said, "I don't f***ing care." He had a lot on his plate. So, she came.

While all this was happening, Cody's mom was trying to stay positive and hold his left hand because they had to cover his whole right hand with a club to prevent him from pulling out any tubes. He had a habit of doing this. Every day, his mom would say positive things to him. She was emotional and showed him all kinds of love daily, holding onto his left wrist and hand. After some days of doing that, the hand and wrist that his mom and others were touching and holding swelled a lot. Eventually, the doctors figured out that his whole left wrist and hand were completely shattered and destroyed. Not from them touching and holding it, but rather from the fall. They had to do surgery for that as well. Before they could, he had to be stable for other things first. It was a catastrophic mess. After all this played out, I returned to Arizona for about a week maybe a week and a half.

In this surgery, they put metal plates and screws into his left hand and wrist to help the bones heal correctly. Then I rented a car and packed a bag this time. With this rental car, I drove back to San Diego and was there for around a week, maybe two weeks. This was the time when he was going out of the beginning stage of intensive care and into the middle stages of intensive care. This was great because there was another bed in this new room, so someone could stay overnight when anyone wanted to stay. I would sometimes take a shift from his mom, and I would stay since, at this point Bridget was pretty much living at the hospital.

This was great because she could finally get some much-needed sleep. During this stage, doctors would come and check his breathing, and they would take him off the breathing tube for three minutes at a time daily to help him learn to breathe again on his own eventually. At this point, Mitch had returned to Maryland to work on deciphering things with Cody's brothers in Maryland and the rest of the family.

I remember the first few days that Mitch and I were together; we were relentlessly making fun of Devin, Cody's oldest half-brother because his girlfriend had recently cheated on him. This was Devin's first love, of course, he was very upset about it. Devin also came to visit at the hospital to get away while he was going through his heart-break. Subsequently, Mitch took Devin back with him to MD. Then Mitch could work on getting everything sorted out. Remember that his youngest brother, Shane, was in high school and Devin had just graduated.

I was back in Scripps again for around two weeks

and then there was a five-day stand where I returned to Arizona. I then returned to San Diego, just spending time with Cody, his family, and the nurses at the hospital. This was when he started to get back to life. When his eyes would move for the first time, they would roll back into the back of his head which was big after not moving at all for at least one month. I would eat every day and spend every night at Chad's house. This time was far less eventful because he wouldn't do anything. I know that once a week or day, the doctors would come in and see how his eyes were reacting to the light they would shine in his eyes. After that week and a half, I went back to Arizona after spending time between the hospital in San Diego and my work in Arizona. I realized I could not focus well on anything at work because he and I were as close as two friends could be. We were attached to the hip for so many years. Of course, I couldn't focus on work. My mental state was not great. It makes sense. Right? Imagine if it were you. You know, the worst part was that no one knew how or if he would come out of the coma or what brain damage he had suffered. Not to mention the kind of life he could have after all the severity of this trauma. There were many unanswered questions throughout this. Before he moved to California, we were roommates for the second time. Then he slept with the girl I was into, but I had to come to Cody's aid, not knowing if he would ever come back to life.

When I went to Arizona the last time, I said it was almost like I had also fallen off the cliff. (If I have not expressed this to you before, I apologize for putting you through this, Chris Martin. I am so grateful you stopped your whole life to ensure I didn't lose mine!)

Additionally, at this point the doctors in the hospital in California said there was not much more they could do for him. He had to go to a rehab facility. Brady and Bridget searched for where he could be planted now. The first couple of places they explored were awful. According to Brady, they were places where people go to die. His family was not ready to let him die. Mitch was already working with the social worker at this hospital to find a place for him after the time there expired. Sometime before Mitch had to go back to MD, the doctors gave him the fun job of stretching his legs occasionally, and he remembers that Cody would scream the entire time until the stretching was completed.

12

Mitch Being
Mitch

Mitch was desperately trying to find an air ambulance company so I could fly back to Maryland from the hospital in San Diego, CA. While in California, Mitch explained to the doctors that I would do better around friends and family in Maryland. He fought with them, knowing that I would. Mitch asserted against the doctors' considerations, "I don't really care what you guys say. My son and wife are coming home." Not to mention how awful the post-hospital places there were bad enough to make my mom cry while visiting with Brady. This decision triggered my insurance company to stop paying. Mitch quickly got on the phone with some air ambulance companies. There were two different companies that he could have used. One was more expensive. The first company Mitch contacted was called "Angel Flight," the cheaper one, but there was no chance that my insurance would assist in the payment at the time. So, Mitch called the other company, AMR. The insurance could potentially help with the payment. There was no guarantee that the insurance would pay, but there was at least a chance with this company. My parents decided on the more expensive company, hoping that my state insurance from Maryland would cover any of the price.

Mitch:

"I remember I was in the parking lot at the pool store in Maryland, trying to get the pool cleaned up, sitting in the parking lot, trying to get all this f***ing stuff figured out. Angel Flight was around 23 thousand, and AMR was around 30 thousand. Mitch could not get on the phone with the insurance company after choosing the company they wanted to use. When he finally got them on the phone, they said they would take us back to Maryland. The insurance company refused to reimburse any amount. Mitch was talking to the insurance company on the phone: "What the f*ck are you thinking? If your f***ing kid was on the other side of the f***ing country, you'd pick up your whole f***ing family and

move?!" In Mitch's words, as he was talking to this doctor from the insurance company, he was so flaking mad, "Who the f*ck are you to tell me to drop every f***ing thing?! I have three other f***ing kids. This is what insurance is for when something like this happens." What this meant was that the insurance never reimbursed Mitch. The solution that my family found to help afford this was to create a GoFundMe page on Facebook to donate money. A fun fact that you probably don't know is that Facebook took 18 or 19% of the funds from the donation. Not all the money donated goes to the purpose of the GoFundMe page. Most of my family made considerable donations, and many good friends and their families did, which immensely helped. I have no words to thank all of you who did this for me and my family. This was the first year Mitch can remember that he got a tax refund in his adult life, and he couldn't even enjoy it. My parents spent all their savings to get me home. Mitch helped many people when he was making a lot of money with his business, and these people did not forget his generosity. They were happy to help him and his family.

A plan took shape when Mitch got word that he had the plane available. The next struggle for him, my loved ones, and even some friends were paying for the whole thing. As you know, an air ambulance, which is so cleverly named, is costly to fly from the southern coast of California to the middle of Maryland. For those unfamiliar with the air ambulance, it's what it sounds like an ambulance for long travel with all the medical amenities found in a typical emergency vehicle or ambulance with a pilot and just enough room for my mom and me. As Mitch always does, he somehow got the money from family and those who donated to get me back to Maryland. He quickly paid the family back. As he always does. I was on my way back home with my mom. I was pretty drugged out for the flight for a good reason."

Let's backup though…

Before I could fly home, Mitch had to go through some agony to get me to a place where I could do rehab and recover. This was a tall order because I had a lot of problems that prevented me from gaining access to most therapy places. First off, I was fed through a feeding tube, which some places would not accept. Then, there was the fact that I was very combative and could not control my body at all. Because of this fact, I had a club over my right hand. I had a very extensive surgery on my left hand and wrist, so my left hand was calm. I would always move a lot in bed, and I would sometimes even pull out my tubes with my right hand without knowing. Thus, the club. There were many concerns for these main reasons. I was always denied at the rehab facilities. Mitch and the Scripps Memorial Hospital social worker were trying their hardest to find me a place in our Maryland area to do rehab. A few weeks passed, and the social worker got no responses from the multiple emails she sent. Naturally, Mitch was growing concerned and realized there must be something wrong. He came to find out that the system that Scripps was using to send the referrals was an old system that was no longer in use. Upon learning this news, Mitch and the social worker went back to work. The email to the closest rehab facility to my small town in Maryland finally received the referral and the rest as they say, is history. Things finally worked. He should get an award or something for the things Mitch went through to get me home. That is just Mitch.

At this same time, Flutie went into extreme introspection, asking himself, "Am I doing what I want to do in my life right now?" Eventually, he had a sit-down conversation with his boss and told him that he would take two weeks off and return to Maryland.

I was getting flown back to Maryland after my time at Scripps had come to an end. Being the best friend, a person could have, he moved back to Maryland and left his job in Arizona. The first few days after Flutie's flight, I had not arrived yet. When I arrived, he visited me at Golden Living Center. It was like my first or second day, and he stayed the whole day. He remembers that.

How I was admitted into rehab at Golden Living Center in Westminster, MD from Tina

Tina: "I don't remember the date, but I had stepped into the role of Golden Living admissions director in Westminster, Maryland. I received a phone call from a social worker/case manager from a hospital out in California. She and asked me if I had received the referral for Cody. I thought this would probably be a bad referral that no one else is taking, and we from Golden Living probably don't want this either.

The social worker told me that the family lives in Carroll County and has a son, aged 25, who recently moved to California. He had gone hiking and fell off the edge of a 50-foot cliff. She had said there wasn't much hope for this young man and that the family wanted him back in Maryland. The caseworker continued to say that he had been recently intubated but was now breathing on his own, had a feeding tube, and had seizures from a traumatic brain injury. She said she had tried every rehab facility in Maryland that she could find and that no one had responded.

Being the mother of two boys, the story tugged at my heart. I had the social worker fax the referral; this would tell us more about him. I was not sure our director of nursing (Cathy Dewitt) would allow us to transfer you to us, but I had to ask. Cathy is an excellent nurse with a lot of critical care background, and she took an interest in his case personally. She was like, 'Let's do this, Tina.'

I reached out to his family to learn more. Then, the next day or two we worked hand in hand with the social worker in California and Mitch to arrange transportation to have him flown into our local airport in Westminster (this was to make the transfer easier and save time). They had an ambulance waiting for him at the airport. In the meantime, the team at Golden Living had decided on a room for Cody. We also knew that being a TBI, we would need the whole room for any equipment.

I wasn't there when Cody arrived late that night, but I know our Director of Nursing, Cathy Dewitt, had stayed to welcome Cody and personally oversee his care. From the stories I heard about him, he had several seizures, and he threw his legs over the bed because of his acuity. We made exceptions that we had never done before to allow family members to spend the night.

It was the best decision we made. Not only did they assist in his care, but they did help us by giving him around-the-clock care. I believe that his family and friends aided in this recovery."

I cannot thank you enough, Cathy Dewitt, Tina, and the entire Golden Living Center team, for taking a chance on me and giving me a second chance at life. I will never forget your kindness and the opportunity you provided me. My whole life could have been completely changed if not for this amazing gesture. I love you all and the entire team.

As all the therapists and nurses had already been informed, I would be admitted to Golden Living Center from California to Maryland, and each center member had an idea of what they were in for. Jay, the lead occupational therapist on the team, read the medical report, and it didn't look good.

It looked like, what they call in the business "a train

wreck". Jay thought: *"well, maybe it won't be as bad as it looks on the record. When he first arrived, he must've been drugged for the long flight and was pretty out of it. When I first came to evaluate him, he was pretty much nonverbal except for crying out. He also could not follow any of my requests. He wasn't really moving. I was thinking to myself, this poor kid. He's not going to get much better than this."*

The next day or the day after. I came into work and learned he had fallen during the night because he tried to get up and walk. Wow, this kid is proving us wrong already. He provided us with a much-needed challenge at the time."

13

Slowly Waking

Up

My first memory after the costly flight from San Diego to Maryland was not until a few days after I had arrived at Golden Living Center.

My rehabilitation center, there was a very nice perpetual old-person home with excellent nursing and rehab programs, which I desperately needed. I was transported immediately from the very close and small airport in Westminster, Maryland to the rehab place via ambulance, also in the same city. Since I had to be so drugged up for the flight, I have no memory of being in Maryland at all for a few days. Or maybe a week. I am not sure of the timeframe.

The first thing I can remember is the first time I had a visit from Uncle Billy and his whole family. If you remember, he is the pastor of a non-denominational church in West Chester, PA. This situation confirmed the mighty power of prayer, with many people praying for me upon hearing the news of the accident.

They chose this opportunity to pray for me during this visit. Throughout all these prayers, I started sobbing. This was the first time I truly understood the gravity of the situation. The first time I consciously realized something happened and how dire the situation would be from this point forward; I didn't understand how demanding and challenging this conscious effort would be.

While the rehab staff took care of me, Mitch was getting to work on my financial future. Since I had survived in the background, unbeknownst to me, he had a new struggle on my behalf again. As if he needed anything more to deal with. Unmoving, this is precisely where Mitch has always thrived. This was no exception.

The therapists at Golden Living Center included Jay, the lead OT; Melanie, the lead PT; Donna, the speech therapist; a PT assistant, Karen; an OT assistant, Lynne; and one more PT Linda. They were an incredible team with no idea they were in for the journey of their lives. They did incredible work for me and all their patients! There were a few other therapists, but I didn't spend much time with them. I think the therapists I worked with the most were Melanie, Karen, Jay, Lynne, and Linda, and the speech therapist Donna, with whom I worked the most.

As far as the nurses, I would have to be near one most of the time, especially at the start. There were a lot of them that helped me throughout my time. The ones that I got the most help from were the super helpful lady named Rhonda, who was always fun. At the start, my primary nurse was named Aisha. The most connected to me was a nurse who went to my high school. She cared for me and became close to me throughout the process. She became a great friend named Melony C. She and I became good friends through this process. We fought like brother and sister. I cannot forget about the nighttime nurses, who were great. Nightly, they would share snacks and water flavoring drops with me. I loved spending time with all the many nurses as I continued with my time throughout. Not only because they helped me with things, I desperately needed help, but they all had very nice and fun personalities. All the nurses, I was very fortunate in this aspect of my rehab, really every aspect.

In that first week, I went from not moving to coming back to life little by little. I was not out of the coma yet. That didn't happen fully for a time. Flutie said he had to fly back to Arizona at some point. I was progressing a lot. Brady was going back to San Diego soon, and Mitch was struggling with his heart stuff. Flutie was thinking about things and wanted someone to be here, hands-on, daily throughout my recovery. So he called his boss and said, "I'm sorry. I'm quitting." He explained the situation, and after the conversation, his boss gave him five grand as severance to help him. This man of his took care of him. They were close. He even donated to get me home. It's funny, but Chris didn't even move yet; all his stuff was still in Arizona. Still, he stayed in Maryland with me, helping me. He even held my penis when I peed and things like that for about a month. I had to pee in a large thermos-looking bottle, much later and had terrible aim as I was getting past using a diaper later. According to my parents and Flutie, as I was coming out of the coma fully, my legs were always flailing, and gosh, my personality was seriously awful. It's not fair, though. I had no control over my emotions, attitudes, conduct, or body. It was very awful for everyone involved. Throughout that first month Flutie kind of realized how difficult and mentally taxing it would be for anyone to be there for me like he wanted to be. My parents were still there, and my mom was still there but Brady was about to return to San Diego in about a month.

Then Flutie canceled his flight back to Arizona to continue helping me. He canceled everything he had going on in Arizona completely. Crazy, I know. He stopped his whole life to care for and support his best friend. He stayed with me for about a month. Then he decided to pack up all his stuff and fully move back to Maryland. Officially. He could see that it would be best for me going forward. He spent almost every day with me for about two months and I'm confident that his being there with me most days had a superior benefit to my recovery. Especially with the rate at which I started improving at Golden Living. They put me in a room with two beds and no roommate. This was the first time they ever put an open bed for family/friend. I had a room to myself. This was because the situation was different from that of other patients, as you can tell. When I was first admitted Flutie was there. He remembers that my legs would go crazy throughout each night. I had terrible restless leg syndrome for weeks; I didn't fully come out of the coma for three weeks after arriving in Maryland. I think this was when I first started coming out of the coma until the doctor of the center put me on a medicine that eventually calmed me, maybe after weeks 3-4. I guess because Flutie had no job at first he had the joy of staying with me overnight when I gave him no chance to sleep the nights he had to stay. Flutie said this was only for around a month, maybe two. There were a few overnight nurses who were very helpful too. At first, he was my roommate once again, but in very different circumstances. I can only imagine how crazy that was to watch, maybe even scary. Flutie says I would freak out throughout the night, and he had to wake me up. When he did, my eyes would roll into the back of my head, which was scary. Probably having a seizure. Then I was back to sleep. That was one of his bedtime jobs to wake me up when I freaked out, as well as fixing the bolsters that attempted to prevent me from moving or falling out of bed, which proved unsuccessful nightly, and fixing my blankets throughout the night because I was always cold. My brain could no longer control my body temperature, so I was always cold!

This was a call to arms for him. Thankfully for me and the nurses during the night, according to Flutie this only lasted 1-2 months, and then he could sleep again. Also, he tells me that I would wake up in a horrible flaking mood every day. After a brain injury, your personality can change quickly and for no reason. I was not intentionally being mean. I had no control over the matter. It is a very common problem after brain injuries, especially when there is damage to the frontal lobe. I was never angry or mean to anyone, if I was working out usually fixed the problem. This time, I had no control over my personality or emotions for longer than I am proud of. To this day, as

I'm recalling right now sometimes my mood changes for no real reason. I'm working on it. It still happens, but not nearly as often or severely as back then. I think I was so angry because of the confusion and frustration as to why I was confused. I didn't know what I had done to my future and life. I didn't know what I was in for yet. I had no idea of the gravity of my situation for some time. I would quickly learn. Even though my best friend had come to my aid, it was a while before I realized what I had just done to myself, and that Flutie was even there.

Remembering when I first realized he was there with me is incredibly difficult. Upon arriving at Golden Living, the first few days or maybe even weeks, are still a blur.

He tells me that when I came back to Maryland, I was not fully conscious and not out of the coma. He says that a lot of the time, I would be looking at him, make eye contact, make a noise. Then, my eyes would look to the left, and I would slowly fade into the distance. This happened a lot in the hospital in San Diego and the first weeks at Golden. The way Flutie explains it, I was slowly coming out of the coma the first few days, but so slowly. Almost becoming conscious again, but not. It is sometimes a slow process to come out of a coma. In my case, it was. Flutie said that I made considerable improvements daily as I became more conscious but was still wildly out of control. My body was active, but my brain was not there. At this juncture, Flutie first felt the fear:

"There's a chance he could be stuck in this state for the rest of his life."

It's crazy because in every state, he would think, "Man, when will he get better, or will he not be able to?"

According to Flutie and others, it took around three weeks for me to fully come out of the coma. To fully understand the things that Flutie would say to me. It took pretty much three weeks to fully come out. Not to mention having some control over my body again, consciously. He says it took at least three weeks after coming back to Maryland. My body was still active, but my brain was not there. After these three weeks, he could finally tell me that I could start to understand when he spoke to me. I could understand what was happening at the moment. He said, "it was like watching a baby go from a newborn to four years old in eight months."

Every day, I would ask him to send a long message to Holly, my longest-standing past relationship. When he didn't, I would get furious at him. As far as texting was concerned, I could not text. So, he and I would go through the many messages on my phone every night. Flutie would help me respond to them around dinnertime. I could not eat just through a tube. This was also before I could. Speak at all. It must have been difficult for him to decipher my thoughts. He also had the job of managing all my friends. Mitch was doing all the logistics. Many friends wanted to see me and talk to me. Eric Holderman was there a lot but didn't do well when he saw me emotionally. I knew that at the time. I enjoyed it every time I saw him. Of course, I never knew this at the time, but Eric had such a difficult time seeing me emotionally. Flutie had to tell him, "Man, if it's too hard for you to deal with this, then don't come visit." He didn't understand that I didn't need him as much as he thought I did. He sucked it up, though and kept coming anyway. I still remember how excited I was every time I saw him. Through this whole process, Flutie could see the rawness of his heart and that it was very vulnerable too.

I can remember what my daily schedule was like back then. I would sleep until around 10:30 or 11:00, and a nurse would always be the first to see me after a night. I would never go the whole night without calling for a nighttime nurse at least once. More like at least twice each night, especially in the early days; there was Aiche, Melony, C., or maybe Rhonda. Whichever of the nurses worked that day. I don't remember much for the first few days or even a week or two. I do remember that it was not until many months into my recovery that I finally had my feeding tube removed from my stomach and my abdominal wall. Until this time, I ate and drank everything from a tube. I can say that the feeding tube scar is the deepest and gnarliest from the accident. That or my left wrist. I know that I came to Golden with a feeding tube in, my hair shaved, and nonstop movement, especially my legs. I can only imagine what the other patients thought upon seeing me come in. According to my speech therapist, Donna, who eventually taught me how to eat and drink again, she told me that it was a very gradual process to get eating again. As was each step of this path, advancing from eating and drinking nothing to eating soft foods and drinking thin liquids. Then, eventually eating enough to get adequate nutrition and hydration. This process took many months until I got that all under my belt.

I can still remember the feeling of waking up in the morning and filling up my pee bottle with the help of my awesome nurses or Flutie. Good times. When I had the urge to evacuate my bladder, someone would help me direct my little wiener into a huge plastic cup, almost like a thermos without a top. This was my only way to pee since I could not walk or stand. I was not able to move from bed. I was in diapers for many months. I know, it's embarrassing. When I was ready for number 2. I would tell everybody, yelling, "It is happening." I guess it's just to prepare the nurses or something I have no idea, once I learned to speak.

As I became more alert and vocal, I eventually could pee into the thermos. It took me a while to get there, and Flutie always helped me aim at first. What could I do though? My speech therapist, Donna, was the first therapist to work with me every day. The day would start with working with Donna. She said that we started working on just following the simplest directions. Jay says he had little faith when he first saw me the least confidence in what they could do with/for me. First, the doctors in California, and then Jay here. They had faith only because I had youth on my side. I was not too young when I had the brain injury at age 24, and I was 25 when I was admitted to Golden for my recovery. Still, my age was crucial for me going forward. When I started working with Donna, I could not speak or communicate. Nothing. Until she taught me to shake my head yes or no. I also could not eat or drink anything. Before I could speak, and after becoming more consciously aware, Brady explained what had happened.

While Donna worked with me hard to regain my voice and have me talking again, Karen and the other physical therapists worked hard to regain my physical parts. Unquestionably, the most impaired part of my brain was in my physical areas of the brain. It was a very tall order for the therapists. I couldn't have asked for a better team! Karen tells me that at first, she was working on me moving in bed and just looking back. I had to relearn everything completely wild, I know. Next, they worked with me on sitting balance. I lacked trunk (butt) stability because I could not hold myself up on my own at all. I used a Hoyer lift to move from the bed to a different place because I didn't have enough muscle to move on my own. This was an excellent tool for me and my recovery. Jay said his only goal when he first evaluated me was for me to sit on the side of the bed on my own, like a newborn baby. It was like learning anything else, but I remember the first few weeks were the hardest. I'm sure you can imagine. The first things that Donna had me work on were elementary things with which I could start to express myself, like learning to shake my head yes or no and simply pointing to things. Next, she started working with me on saying the whole words "yes and no." Like I said, it took months, maybe 4-6.

14

No Pain, No Gain

Once I could say yes and no, I subconsciously knew I would speak again. She gradually made the types of questions she asked harder, like multiple-choice. She would ask me, "Do you want milk or juice?" Questions that only had one correct response. Then, gradually the questions became more complex. For example, "What meal do we eat in the morning?" Finally, to open-ended questions that can't be answered with a single word (Why should we hire you?). While Donna was re-teaching me how to speak, Karen and the other PTs were busy re-teaching me how to use my body with whatever muscle I had left in my 135-pound body. I was around 185 before my coma with a nice muscle tone a little difference in weight and muscle build, as you could surmise. Eventually, I could move my body in bed to continue working towards waking up my tiny legs and muscles the same size as my mom's wrist, and she is not a big lady. I would get rolled around in a rolling chair after using the Hoyer lift to strengthen my legs to get to the therapy room. I was training my little skinny legs again to stand up again. I can only envision how much more arduous this growth would have been if I had never taken steroids in the past. The doctors in California said that if my neck had not been so strong, I likely would have been paralyzed in the fall. My large neck muscles acted like a splint for my spine and prevented it from being severely severed or damaged. It all comes around, doesn't it? I am not condoning steroids, though every single set of neck exercises, "neckerixes," was not for nothing. I didn't get to utilize them for football. I used them for something far more important.

Every morning, after my speech therapy, which Flutie would help with, Karen and the other PT therapists put me on the motorized exercise bike to get my legs engaged again. I started working on the motorized bike before I was able to stand. I couldn't speak yet, either when working on the bike or doing other things I had to do to get my legs back to functioning. I was very grateful to still be alive without knowing how close to my bitter end I was yet. I was confident, subconsciously at least, that I would eventually be able to stand up on my own with the help of the recovery family, as well as with the support of my actual family and friends. I had always loved challenging myself, and this would be the largest one of my life. It was going to be incredibly difficult for my body and mind, not to mention my disconnected brain.

As Donna taught me to speak again, Karen, Linda, and Melanie, the physical therapists worked hard to help me use my legs again. It's kind of crazy how I had such extreme restless leg and arm syndrome, and I had completely lost control of my extremities after the coma. I had almost no muscle anymore, so how could I move my extremities so often? It was all involuntary. Linda tells me my extremities moved so much without enough muscle to move my body. It's most curious. She tells me that it was like I could not relax my body at all when I first arrived for a while.

All my therapists had their work cut out for them. The first step was to start working with me on being able to move in bed alone. It had to have been incredible to watch from the view of the therapists with me coming in the place with my head half shaved, my body completely out of control with no ability to speak or follow the simplest of directions, with my 135lb frame. I guess only my family and Flutie knew how much I loved challenging myself, and this was the largest of challenges. Each day would probably start the same for the first few months. I would wake up after not a very restful night of sleep, get some nutrition from a bag right into my stomach and then my therapy would start speech with Donna teaching me and Flutie's help. I continued to get better slowly. After my speech therapy each morning, I learned to sit up independently. I would be transferred from the bed into a rolling reclining chair. With naps after each therapy, I was not yet able to sit up on my own. After my therapy each morning I would stay in the recliner to make it easier for when the nurses needed to come to me. I was getting better at moving on my own in bed. They next worked with me to put my feet on the floor from the height of the bed. This was already more improvement than Jay thought I could ever accomplish. That's OK, Jay. I know how bad I looked when I arrived. I don't hold it against you. This is a very interesting process for me now. I started to learn about all the tasks that my therapist had to go through as I went through them. On the other side. For instance, my legs did not stop going crazy at first, which means that my therapists had to work with me with my legs not being able to stop moving. What a sight to see. I have no idea what it looked like as the multiple therapists struggled to move me from the bed and to the rolling chair with the help of a Hoyer medical lift every day for weeks, with my legs and arms flailing the entire time. I had no idea what a Hoyer lift was or what it looked like until I started writing this. There are some very good pictures of what it looks like and how it works on Google or any search engine. For those who know anything about brain injuries, one of the most prevalent symptoms is extreme fatigue which I still fight with every single day. It was much worse at the onset of the injury. My therapists told me that I had only enough energy for one half-hour therapy session at a time, and then I needed to rest or nap again. Brady remembers that one of the first physical therapy exercises they had me do was incredibly simple but not for the therapist. I guess after being in a coma for two months and not moving my legs at all for that much time, my hamstrings were so incredibly tight. They had to stretch them every day, and

I would scream, moan, and make awful noises. So much pain. It was essential on the off chance I could use my legs fully again.

Donna was usually the first therapist to see me in the morning. She remembers how, sometimes it was tough for her to keep me awake for the whole 20 minutes, especially in the beginning. It was not a great time for the therapists helping me at the facility. Between my aggravation, controllable movements, fatigue, and my very short attention span. It got better in time as I completely became conscious. Still, at the start it was very difficult for me and my therapists. After one or two weeks, as I was trying to regain control of my body after not using it at all for months, including four brain surgeries, it was time to see what I could do with my new body.

I'm sure that many people have different stories, but this was mine. Around this time, my legs slowly started to calm down from the restless leg syndrome. Nighttime was a great time for my family and Flutie, as I was starting to calm down overnight. I know it was a suggestion of the Golden Living doctor, Dr. Middleton to start me on medicine to calm my legs, and it worked like a charm. I love this man.

This was when things started coming together for me and my recovery. I could not yet speak sentences, and Donna was pushing me with her therapy while the physical stuff with the others was pushing me the rest of the day. One day, I was working with Karen, and Donna was there too. They were working with me, putting my feet on the floor by myself for the first time. This was a big deal at the time. I was always aggravated by trying difficult things, and my mood wasn't the best. The therapists were very excited about the improvements that were coming.

While I was trying hard to put my feet on the floor,

my bad attitude got the better of me, and I ended up yelling, "You bitch" at Karen due to the pain, both physical
and mental, I was experiencing. This was my first sentence
after learning to speak again. By this point, I could only say
a few words. The combination of my aggravation and the
pain somehow gave me the ability to speak my first complete sentence since the hospital in California, of which I
have no memory. Not exactly the best first full sentence,
but all the therapists couldn't have been prouder and more
excited. I was improving more and more. I could finally
put my feet on the floor, and my speech started coming as
the days continued. Flutie started having more of a role in
my recovery taking control of all the friends who wanted to
visit me while I was going through therapy. As my recovery
continued, only my closest friends. I wasn't ready to show
myself to everyone just yet. Maybe one day I could walk
and speak or converse again as I enjoyed so much before.
It was my favorite pastime, just talking to people and I was
good at it. Whether at the gym, in random public places,
or with the waiter at a restaurant, I always met people and
loved it. For this reason, I knew most of the members of my
home gym in Hampstead, MD.

I met and became best friends with Zauhn. The first
friend who came to see me before I could even form sentences while still in a diaper was Cinamonthia. I remember
this so well because I remember pooping or something in
my diaper while spending time with her. Or at least flatu-
lating severely with her not ever mentioning it. It was very
sweet of her. I would have done the same in the same situation. Whether or not I did anything in my diaper, I appreciated her coming to see me early into my rehab. It was a
few weeks before I had my next Golden Living visitor as I
continued my demanding therapy.

I was getting better with my speech little by little, and I was on my way to relearning to answer simple questions with only one correct answer. While I continued fighting with Karen and the other physical therapists daily as they were simply doing their jobs, it was not my intention to be difficult. This was where I was. This was around the two-week mark, after which I had significantly improved. With so much to relearn, by this time, I could put my feet on the floor with no help. I was on my way to getting my scrawny legs back to life, which I desperately needed. It might feel small, but it was huge the first step to standing again. When I was home in Maryland, my legs, my mom says, were the same size as her wrists and she is not a thick woman. To strengthen these weak things, my physical therapists started putting me on some leg machines in the therapy room in conjunction with using the motorized bike. At the same time, Jay and the other OTs were busy doing their thing. I can imagine it was not much with my left wrist being indisposed. Since I had extreme reconstruction surgery on my left wrist, I must've tried to catch myself with my left hand in the fall, which didn't work well. Hence the surgery.

The doctor tasked with fixing my wrist had to put a few metal parts together to piece my wrist together again. Like I said, I don't think it was a lot of fun for the OTs. All the therapists worked together on my case. It was all hands-on deck the first few months or so. I'm sure the priority was getting me as close to walking again as possible. Since no one had any idea if that would be in the cards or not, they started teaching me how to use a wheelchair once I was able to support myself after lots of practice, and I hated using it. The physical therapists trained me little by little; they started by having me move through all the different body movements, helping a lot at the start, then gradually less. I'm not exactly sure when they started this. When I could speak again, I always asked Flutie to see if I could talk with

Holly, my ex-girlfriend. It was very weird and annoying for him. It was every day for a while. For some reason, it was almost like my brain was returning to that past relationship like I was still in it. Maybe because she was the closest I had been to love. At the same time, I was strengthening my muscles, core, arms, and legs aside from the omni cycle and the motorized workout bike to wake up my legs. I started with laying down exercises with support, then rolling, crawling, kneeling, sitting with support, sitting up with support, then without support, standing with support. Then, I finally stood on my own with no help. This was about my first six months at Golden Living. As far as my physical therapy was concerned. I was doing well, but I still had a long way to go. Like the learning process of a baby, but at age 25. While my legs and core were strengthening and I was slowly learning to use my body, I was still learning from Donna how to speak and eventually eat again. Only in the telling of this part did I understand that a person can still eat with a feeding tube in. I don't exactly know when I had it removed, but before that day could come, I had to go through some more therapy with Donna. It may surprise many of you reading this that speech therapy includes eating and swallowing. That was all news to me. It was teaching a huge baby, me. I'm pretty sure that some severe TBI victims go through something similar in their rehab journey. Right now, as I am writing this, it has been around five years since I was at this rehab center. I apologize if I can't get all the specifics.

By the time I could stand on my own, I was off to the races. My rehab started to speed up significantly and didn't stop. Not only physically but also in my speech. Even my relearning to eat and swallow improved at a quicker pace. This could have been because I understood what I could accomplish by continuing to push. Or because this was around the time that the doctor put me on Adderall or both. I was finally making significant upturns weekly. I arrived at Golden Living in August 2016. It was almost winter. In the first six months, I first stood up on my own and spoke my first sentence. I was improving my speaking and was learning to eat slowly (with my parents sneaking me ice cream sundaes).

My mom remembers how much I loved the whipped cream. Strangely, the cuss words were flowing. The craziest part of this was before this life-changing accident. I very rarely, if ever, said bad words. For some reason, I would cuss at everyone, especially when the nurses or therapists would feed me. I was relearning to eat little by little. It's a common occurrence with damage to the frontal lobe of the brain, which I suffered brutally. I distinctly remember that once I could stand on my own, the therapists first started working with me on balancing on the parallel bars. These were bars with a mat in between for safety purposes. These sessions always involved multiple therapists to help me move through these bars safely and correctly. My new schedule was like this: wake up, do speech therapy with Donna, do my physical therapy in the parallel bars, and work out and OT. Then cussing at the nurses as they tried to feed me once I could speak. I apologize for my bad attitude, as everyone was trying to teach me. I'm unsure why I was such a jerk each time, but Mitch remembers it like yesterday. I was not very nice.

Speaking of having a poor attitude, I gave the worst of it by far to Flutie. I wish that I hadn't. He is one of my best friends. He stopped his whole life to come to my aid. I wish I had any control over my emotions back then. I'm very indebted to him. This was right around the time that Abby came to visit me at Golden Living. I didn't expect that I would have her come to visit. Especially because we didn't keep in touch much after my move to California with me being entirely at fault. Regardless she must have liked me more than I ever realized. She tells me that at this point in my recovery, around January 10. I could converse in complete sentences. I'm sure it wasn't great, but I was there. Now, with my most recent lover by my side, I didn't understand her feelings for me and how strong they were until she first came to see me there. Then, I still didn't realize. I also didn't realize that she would be back. Knowing how far the drive to come and see me was. Not to mention that most of the friends who would come to visit would stop by for a few hours, put a few pictures on social media, and not come back. Which I appreciated each time, but this annoyed Flutie a lot. Abby was different. Not only did she come back after driving from outside of Philadelphia, which was not very close to my rehab place in a suburb of Baltimore, but she came weekly.

I never saw her home, but I knew it was close to Philly. It must have been important to her to make that trip for little ol' me. According to her memory, I could speak but couldn't walk. Flutie was still pushing me daily, even when my attitude was awful and I would exclaim, "I don't want to do this." Still, he stayed with me, thrusting me back to the correct state of mind. This was like a full-time job for him as these thoughts hit often, especially at the start. He kept me in line the whole time, especially watching me go from one to one hundred in the blink of an eye which I still struggle with today. Not nearly as bad. Speaking with Abby, I learned much about why she did what she did for me. But let's back up real quick.

I spoke with her and learned I did not make the best first impression upon meeting her. Once I finished my set with the band, I began thanking some girls who showed up by buying them drinks, regardless of age or not. Abby's first thought, in her own words, "Who is this loser buying underage girls drinks?" That was me. I guess I was lucky that she was attracted enough to my stage moves. They were sufficient to make up for my awful first suspicious actions. This first view of me didn't stop her from eventually falling for me. As you can realize at this point, in reading thus far, I was incredibly lucky and blessed to have this helpful, selfless, and caring girl in my corner too. It is interesting, but I didn't know too much about her compassionate nature before. I was soon to find out. The first day that she came to see me, I was happy. Flutie met her for the first time, as well as my parents. I imagine it must've been nerve-wracking for her. She held it together and got it done. I was excited when she came to see me for the first time. I was ecstatic when she came back the following weekend. For the next few weeks, I had Flutie with me most days. Eric occasionally, and Abby every weekend. Sometimes, different friends visit, and my parents visited from time to time. Since Abby worked during the week, she could only come on the weekends which was always great for me. I know Abby was not my girlfriend, but she may well have been.

As I continued with my therapy, I could finally stand on my own. With this huge step, I started to work with therapy, standing for larger amounts. Then, eventually, I moved my weak legs with the help of a walker and the therapists. This was a process of around four weeks. While I was also learning how to move around in a wheelchair just in case, I couldn't learn to walk fully again. I was learning at a quick pace. I didn't realize it then. Looking back, I can see it now. After these four weeks, I was able to speak better and was improving with using my muscles in such games as cornhole. I have a video on my YouTube channel of Flutie helping me play cornhole one time, and you can see what I said about being mean to him while helping me with this therapy. It was not great for my best friend, who was desperately trying to help me recover from this terrible situation. I was such a huge jerk to him when I was trying to use my muscles like playing cornhole, which had a lot to do with the fact that I just had very little control of my body. I was fully aware of the difficulties with my legs, but with my upper body, I had the idea that my upper body still worked well. I realized that I was mistaken. I had to just keep swimming like Dory in "Finding Nemo." Also, like Nemo, I would ask the same questions repeatedly once I could speak. My recovery was going much better than expected, and I wasn't done. By the time Abby came, I was eating real food. I just needed to be fed. Most times I ate, I would hear it from Donna for eating too fast. My response was always the same. I had to eat fast; I have three brothers. I still had my feeding tube in until I was good at eating and swallowing. When I started eating real food, I had to poop more, a struggle in itself especially aiming my butt into the seat to poop into the hole. There was one day when I went to go poop in the toilet, missed the hole and pooped right onto the side of the seat. We called this doing a number 3. I don't remember if this was before or after I started eating real food but when I started learning to poop and sans diaper. By the time I was eating real food I had begun to work out very lightly with the therapists to help me, from the large, motorized chair to the various machines. Most of the therapy time was used to wake up my legs and start helping me walk again. I think at this point that most of the therapists and my family, I guess, as well as Flutie, knew that I would be walking again one day. I was excited about the idea. Each day after my breakfast and speech therapy, I spent considerable time going to the therapy room to work out my legs on the bike and then practicing walking in the parallel bars with one therapist, usually, two or three to help me learn to walk.

I don't remember what the situation was, but one time I was in the therapy room with Melanie and Mitch, and I had the urge to pee very bad. Mitch and Melanie helped me to the bathroom. I couldn't hold it or control my body well yet, and I peed on both of them. It happened more than once. As I was learning to walk again I would need at least three therapists to help me move from the chair to start my work, which made things worse. It was hard for me to go from the chair to standing. That was my first challenge before I could even work on walking. I could fully converse by this time, but my filter was gone. Mitch and my mom had to remind me often to use my filter. If something came to mind, I could not control whether I said it or not. This was a problem I had for at least two years.

I remember after I learned to eat again. Mitch often brought me milkshakes, which the therapists were not very excited about. He loves to stretch the rules. I know when I started to eat independently; my extreme need for coffee came into play. I became super addicted to coffee excessively. Before this accident, I drank it once a day. As my therapy wore on, my brain and body, especially my brain, were exceptionally exhausted all day and all night until sleep. I got to the point where I would drink around 6-8 cups of coffee each day to keep the fatigue at bay after I stopped Adderall. Bless his heart, Flutie. Every day he visited, he would bring me a coffee. Right around the same time, I had walked alone without help in the parallel bars. I started with my coffee consumption. Again, I have a video of this first walk without help on my YouTube channel. I don't think I drank any coffee until I could walk or walk well, or at least without being watched carefully by the therapists. I don't remember the time frame from when I could only stand on my own to when I first walked. Flutie, Mitch, and

I all remember how it was as I was getting close to walking. After walking my first steps, I continued my therapy daily. Once I knew that walking was a possibility for me again, I was more inspired than ever to walk without help. A display of what life could one day be. I wanted to return to the fun things I loved so much in my first life. Which indeed included walking. I don't exactly remember, and no one else seems to either, but at some point, as I was getting close to walking on my own Mitch had something to do for a few days, so he could not come to see me at Golden. It must have been the craziest thing for him when he returned to Golden to see me after those few days. I had improved so much that I could take my first steps without help. Flutie was so excited to show Mitch that he rode me in the wheelchair to the hallway. When he arrived, I could show him I could walk a couple of steps on my own. Needless to say, he was very shocked, impressed, and proud. Maybe even a little bit confused. "What the f*ck happened when I was gone?" I think he exclaimed. "What the f*ck!"

Once I could walk a little, I could come home for the first time for the weekend. At this point, Flutie realized I would make a remarkable recovery—not exactly back to normal, but much better than anyone thought. It was about that time to try going home for a weekend since I had already improved to walking a couple of steps without help, eating on my own, and going to the bathroom without assistance. Of course, sometimes I still needed help with some of those things. I was improving rapidly, though I had the hardest time sitting in chairs, and walking through doors as I still do. I cannot forget about this. As I'm reliving these days, Holly Berry came one day and brought me a Keurig machine so I could have an easy way to have an unlimited amount of coffee daily. This was huge for me. Flutie also remembers that I could never eat enough. The doctor said

I should eat a lot to heal my brain and body. This was also a big game-changer for me. He remembers that I could eat a whole pizza and still be hungry. At this point, I could not use the Keurig machine on my own. Throughout each day, I had to ask the therapist to help me feed my desire for coffee many times a day.

As I continued improving my walking and steadiness, the therapists helped me relearn how to walk on hills, different terrains, and ground levels. Then, as far as walking was concerned, my most significant challenge was walking up stairs. Eventually, this took the most time. My parent's house had two sets, including the upstairs that led to my brother's rooms and mine. Thankfully, my parents had the thoughtfulness to make Mitch's office my new room, which was on the first floor, so I didn't need to use the stairs to get to my room. Thanks again, Mitch. I must exclaim that conquering the stairs was no easy task for me physically, emotionally, or for the therapists due to my frustration.

Immediately after, I was fully able to eat real food again. At least six months after arriving at Golden, Mitch took me to eat at Friendly's that day. For those who don't know Friendly's, it is the MD version of DQ. So, we ate a lot of unhealthy but delicious food for my first restaurant visit since the accident, where I could eat on my own. I had come a long way in these first six or so months. I still had one large trial: walking without any help at all. I always needed someone for support and balance. Now that I could do elementary things, I could finally go home for a weekend. It was a huge thing for me to finally see my dogs and sleep in a different bed at my home, where my brothers, minus Brady, and my parents lived. Once I could eat on my own, the doctor told me that it was very important that I ate as much as possible to get as many calories as possible to heal my brain. I took full advantage of this, eating everything in sight. Every morning, I would wake up and eat whatever breakfast was on the menu at Golden's breakfast that day. I also ate a PBJ after each meal there. 20% of calories consumed are used only to run the brain.

Or Mitch made me French toast at home, a very large portion. Then, Flutie visited with a large cup of coffee in hand. We would work on speech therapy. After that, we would go to the therapy room and I would be greeted by all the patients, sometimes funny ones. I talked with a lot of the other patients. I was the youngest by far. The next youngest patient was a super nice guy named Jeff. He quickly became my closest patient friend. Each day after my speech therapy I would go to the therapy room and see Jeff working on his therapy trying to walk again. He was an older man who experienced a horrible workplace accident. I have to say, from what I saw in those eight months, Jeff and I were the hardest-working patients at the facility. Also, the youngest. That could have been why we came so close. It was very interesting that he and I were told we would never walk again.

He would always talk with me, and we gave each other hope. When Jeff and I became close. He told me that when I first arrived at Golden, his first thought was, "What the hell happened to that guy?" I did not look good. Little did he know, this awful-looking dude would become his closest rehab friend. We exchanged numbers and kept in touch over the years, and wouldn't you know it, he's also walking again now too.

In talking with Abby about this time, she would help me with anything and everything she could, including having me go to the bathroom, spending time with me, and keeping my spirits up whenever possible. I just really needed that from time to time.

Eventually, she even took me into civilization too.

Flutie would get me out more, but doing it with a girl was nice. Also, around that time, I learned to walk again, barely. My therapists let me work out in the therapy room using the machines, which was awesome. It made me feel somewhat normal again since working out was a large part of my life before. Also, they did it to wake up the rest of my body and other muscles that had not worked for too long. Occasionally, I would be graced with Eric's presence. I was always very excited to see him each time he visited, but once I could walk again, I saw him less and less. It made sense to me. He had to get a job, which happened with Flutie too. I could not be mad at Eric at all. I inspired him to come to California with me, which didn't work as planned, at no fault of his own.

This is a strange memory, but a very strong memory was the first time I showered at Golden, having to sit in a chair. It was a huge step for me and a large step for Rhonda, who was my shower nurse. She did everything with me and for me, and I love Rhonda. She was the only one that would shower me the whole time. Regarding my relationship with Abby, Flutie and she got along well. I'm sure that he appreciated all the help she gave me. The girl who treated me the best of all the girls I had been with. It could have been because she liked me the most. When I reached the point where I could walk independently and speak well enough that people could understand me most of the time, Flutie started coming less and less. Still, I would be blessed every weekend with Abby coming to see me. I was still working on therapy multiple times a day, working out, and trying to be the best version of myself-my new self. When I was going through all my therapies and working on walking again, and as I slowly learned to walk better somewhere around this time, I went to the mental therapist at Golden Living. She helped me talk through the extreme trauma I had suffered, dealing with a new life that I had fashioned, creating a plethora of emotions. Some I did understand, others I didn't. This rehab facility had every little facet of rehab that I needed the best therapies of each kind. It was everything that I needed at that time. The problem lay in everything I was good at in my life; I trained for years and years, from working out to playing sports and running to eventually playing guitar and singing in the band. I had to relearn everything that took me so many years before. I must try again with this severely damaged brain. Not to mention a brain that is not in total control of emotions and body. This therapist helped a lot, as much as she could.

15

Almost
Home

I got to the point where I could finally go home for weekends. I was excited to sleep in a bed at my house, a more familiar place. It was cool because I had some time with the dogs too. I got to sleep with them; it was great since I was always cold, and dogs are always warm, especially little Rocco, the Boston terrier. At least once a night in the beginning, twice a night my nighttime nurses at Golden came in when I would complain of being cold. The nurses would either put on more blankets or fix my blankets from my moving throughout the night. I was nowhere near past this when I got to go home for the weekend, but my parents knew about it. Now that there were no nurses to fix my blankets throughout the night but my parents only, I was always cold after the accident. My brain could no longer control my body temperature. I very distinctly remember that the day I was picked up to go home for the first weekend, the therapists and nurses set out a wheelchair for me to take with me for the weekend. Mitch left it on the sidewalk without speaking with anyone, then left with me in the car. This was just his personality.

It was a good thing he did. I never used the wheelchair again. This first weekend home showed me that I did not need the wheelchair anymore. I could not walk well without help. Mitch's exact words were, "Cody, you are not in a wheelchair." So, I wasn't. That's one thing he taught me throughout his struggles with heart disease: if you want it enough and have the strength and will, there is nothing that you can't do. I watched as he went through so many heart surgeries. He just could not give up because he had such a strong and loving family. I felt the same way. I had no choice but to push on. I didn't think about the future at this point. Instead, I only worried about improving daily. Let me be clear: this whole process was not easy. Ever. There were a lot of days when I wanted to give up. The same reasons that Mitch couldn't. I couldn't. I improved throughout the week, and I saw my family at home on weekends. I forgot to mention that Nick Strong and his family visited a few times too. This was a flight from New Orleans to Baltimore each time for Nick. Once he graduated from college, he landed a nice job out there. He didn't leave me during these challenging times, either. Once I got back to Golden, I missed Abby, who would see me at home frequently, but it was nice to be home for the weekend.

It was right back to training for walking, speech, and all the rest of the therapies. I kind of could not wait to continue working on walking. This first weekend away was like a vision of what life could be like if I pushed on with my therapies and walked again on my own. It was after this first weekend that I realized it was not going to be easy. Nothing worth doing ever is. I could eventually get back to a semi-normal existence again. It was back to work at Golden for that to be an actual reality. I proceeded to endure my therapies and learning. The therapists knew that I did not want to use the wheelchair. I focused on trying to regulate my moods. Easier said than done. I felt that I was getting close to my goals. I could already take steps independently, but I was not very confident and had little control over walking. I knew though, that if I continued pushing on with the help of my therapists, I would eventually get there.

I have a very distinct memory of trying to learn how to coordinate my arms to use a wheelchair correctly. It was just as frustrating, or more so, than learning to walk. I think it was because I couldn't coordinate my body and nerves the way I wanted to which I still struggle with today. It was worse and more difficult when I was first doing therapy. It didn't matter. Mitch and I both agreed that I would not be in a wheelchair for the rest of my life. I would walk for the rest of my life. As the therapy progressed, I was trying new things daily to be able to walk without any help a huge goal of mine. As far as the OTs, I still didn't make much use of my left hand. Before I left the hospital in California, they put some metal in my left wrist to put the bones back together as much as they could. I knew at some point I had to get surgery to take the screws and plates out. Before I left California, the doctors told my parents that the screws and plates should be in my wrist for about three weeks for the bones to come back together and heal but due to my insurance, it was closer to six months. When I fell, I must've thought to try to catch myself with my left hand. Regarding my speech, I could speak and converse but sometimes, I would stutter and get stuck on certain words. It still happens today, but it was worse back then. Time is a great medicine. I don't remember when exactly this happened, but at some point during some of my therapy time at Golden, I know that Mitch had a heart attack as he was struggling with heart disease. Since I was drowning in medical bills Devin and Mrs. Berry helped set up a golf tournament to raise money. It was a lot of work for them, but they did it in love. I was currently working on walking on my own with help. I thought this would be my time to shine and show all my followers, friends, and family how far I had come. My goal was to walk on my own during the tournament.

This idea of having this short-term goal inspired me all that much more. I was going to be able to walk on my own the whole time at the tournament. Mark my words; I was going to do it. I continued my therapy with a new sense of urgency. I knew that I could push myself more to meet this goal. When I heard about the golf fundraiser, I couldn't wait to see my friends and family there. I had to learn to walk on my own. I had no choice. I had to do it for everyone who donated to get me here. It was only fitting. This golf tournament was in October it was not super warm in Maryland, but it was nice with all my friends and family being there and all the great food. There was an auction too, creating more fun and donations. I had met my goal by the time the golf tournament was upon us. I was walking on my own on this great day. I arrived, walking slowly with no help. My mom and everyone else were very proud. There was a lot of alcohol and food. When the day ended, we, Brady's friends, and my family continued the party at my house.

The alcohol continued to flow more and more. What I remember the most were two conversations one during the golf outing and one the next day. When I arrived, Sack saw me immediately hugged me tightly, and said that if anyone could make it through something like this, it was you. This sentence has lived in my mind every day since. The second conversation was with Nick Strong, where he explained that he had peed on the couch where he slept after his night of getting a little bit too drunk. He peed on my sleeping spot on the nights I was able to sleep at home since it was close to my parents' room in case I needed anything or when I would get cold and needed more blankets. I didn't even know this at the time because I was with my friends and family for the first time since my accident; I was drinking some beer too. Little did I know how bad alcohol is for a TBI. I didn't learn this for years to come. I would always drink alcohol during social occasions; that was what I did throughout my whole adulthood. I could feel how much more sensitive my brain was to alcohol now. This golf tournament was a great success for me, my family, and my friends. The first time I went out was after being at Golden for eight months. I had made huge improvements in those eight or so months. Dude, I mean, the doctors at Scripps thought I would be in bed the rest of my life. I would never be able to take care of myself, not to mention walk. Like Brady said, "I was defying all odds." I think it was around this time that I realized that everything is possible with enough willpower. It didn't hurt to have great people in my corner: my family, friends, and therapists.

After this incredible weekend, I returned to Golden to continue my therapies and working on strengthening my whole body, especially my legs. I had lost almost all my leg muscles through the coma. It makes sense since I was in bed for at least two months without moving consciously. This facility had a nice therapy room I took full advantage of once I could finally walk around without help. Once I could walk around, I would talk to everyone all day, especially Jeff in the therapy room. It was near this time that the therapists told Flutie that I was going to hit a plateau in my therapy at some point because I made so many huge accomplishments in such a short amount of time. Looking back, it is kind of funny now; it was like watching a baby grow up from a newborn to four years old, even emotionally. As I was doing my life at Golden occasionally, Flutie would take me to get food, coffee, or both to get me out to civilization again. It was always a great time, and gosh, it was hard for me to get in and out of a car. I remember one time that he took me out to get food at a local restaurant called Baughers that we both enjoyed, and he forgot to buckle my seat belt and got pulled over because of it. The people at Golden were very upset. Another memory he has that is very strong is how hard it was for me to walk through doors with my vision problems and something known as proprioception, which is the ability to know where your body is in space. I would not learn about it for years to come.

At this point in my recovery, I was getting much better, but I was still always struggling with fatigue. If I did go out with him, I could only do things within about an hour before my whole body and brain would almost turn off. Not literally, but that's how my mind and body would react. I could no longer speak or walk well until I got some sleep. Approximately the time I could walk on my own again, I was finally able to get surgery on my left wrist. I had to take an ambulance to the hospital, but I couldn't have cared less. I was excited to finally get my wrist fixed. When I left the hospital in California. The surgeons told my parents that in around three weeks, the metal in my wrist should be taken out. As a result, of my insurance woes, it ended up being more like six months until the surgery could be done. It's OK, though; eventually, it was done well in California and Maryland. One of these doctors said my wrist looked like an accordion. Luckily, the trainer who taught me how to work out when I was in 8th grade now owns her own gym, which is not too far from Golden, Dani K. Gym & Wellness. As I improved and could walk comfortably, I worked out with her in her gym until I went home. I enjoyed those times, not only because it helped to strengthen my weakness throughout my whole body but also to go back to something I loved my whole life with my favorite trainer and close friend.

16

He Is

Family

Looking back at how Flutie decided to come to be with me and ultimately come to my aid, he thinks it was mostly an emotional decision because when the accident happened, he still hated me. The last thing he told me before I moved in with Greg was that he never wanted to see me again. I think this was the last thing he said to me after being so attached to me for many years like brothers; he just couldn't leave it at that. Thank God he didn't. I needed him. I didn't have much control over this. I feel so bad that some days I have no memory of him being there with me the day before. It was emotionally rough for him, as you can imagine.

I think even more for him than for me because I was more preoccupied with my therapies and figuring out life again. I think I was much less affected by that than Flutie because I knew I already had the people I needed the most by my side. I realize now that other people have their own lives. It still blows my mind that after getting into a sexual relationship with the one girl that my best friend loved, he still came to my aid when I indeed didn't deserve it. It's very interesting to think about it now that he came to see me all the way in California, a real Christian brother. With the intense story we shared, each day was its own adventure. Sometimes good, sometimes bad. It had to have been very stressful and tiring for eight straight months. He's a strong man, and ladies, he's available.

Through this difficult and frustrating situation, I asked him if he ever thought, "Man, did I make a mistake by doing this?" He said no. Once he left his job in Arizona, he was fully committed. I know that he was very proud each time I made improvements, which would be almost weekly after I fully came out of the coma. He can never forget how much Mitch helped while simultaneously fighting and dealing with his own and other stuff. Every day Mitch came to see me, he always brought food, classic Mitch. Thinking about Flutie's life, it's irrational because his decision to come to my aid put his life on a whole new trajectory. I cannot thank him enough for making that decision. He said each time he would take me out to get ice cream or food, the people working at Golden gave him crap, but I think they knew that he always had my best intentions in mind.

Even when I was with him, he forgot to put on my seat belt. I remember that day because we went to our favorite local restaurant, Baugher's (shout-out), for awesome homemade food. We always ate there before the accident. That was always our spot. I have a strong memory of going to Buffalo Wild Wings with many friends but I couldn't last very long with my extreme fatigue. I was good for about an hour or two if I had coffee. Then, everything would start to shut down quickly. It was also a good thing for him because he got to see some friends and then go back to Baltimore.

He tells me he doesn't talk about this journey with many people because it was just a selfless act he had to do. He doesn't like when people brag about themselves. At the end of the day, I think only he, me, and maybe Mitch, my mom, and Brady will ever fully understand. Really, what's the point of telling others?

Mitch gained newfound respect for Flutie throughout this process, and Flutie gained the same thing for Mitch. It was very encouraging for Flutie to watch me go from extremely close to death to functioning. When I was in a coma at the hospital, the doctor came in and explained my recent MRI, and the doctor explained that only family could be in the room. Mitch said yes, this guy is family. That always made him feel comfortable and at home. He remembers during this talk with the doctor about the MRI that all the dark spots could be permanent damage under all the blood that was surrounding my brain. From seeing the large number of dark spots, he thought I would be a vegetable for the rest of my life. Flutie said that the doctors didn't have much of an idea of what parts of my brain were damaged the most, but there were a lot of dark spots. There was just no way to know. The doctor then explained that after my coma, I could come out as a completely different person with a different personality—my mom's biggest fear. Not to mention that Flutie was a little scared that I would wake up and remember that we weren't on great terms because of the girl stuff, mainly because we never really had any talks about that situation, but like Mitch told him, girls come and go; don't worry about it. It was okay because it was the last thing on my mind. Flutie took his advice by coming to California to be with me during these most difficult times and not leaving until I got home. After eight months at Golden Living, I went home, and Flutie would continue to visit but not as much. It made sense to me. He had to get back to his own life now that I was able to start getting to the point of learning how to take care of myself again. It's not like he left when I got home, but he would come once or twice a week at the start. It was a massive step for me to go home formally.

17

Back Home

Again

Since I was finally coming home, not just for the weekend, Mitch and my mom relocated my room from upstairs to Mitch's office which was on the first floor, safer for me. During the weekend visits, I would just sleep on the couch. This office had a nice bed, a chair, and for visitors, a TV and a computer. I loved this living situation. I finally spent all week with my brothers, parents, and all four dogs. My first few days at home were lovely. On weekends, when I would come home from Golden, Mitch would always make me a large breakfast of French toast. I always loved it and still do. I didn't eat that huge breakfast at home anymore but I still had a great breakfast and a lot of food. As your brain heals from injury, it needs as many calories as possible. Like I said, 20% of the calories you eat are used just to run your brain. I couldn't clothe myself yet and I had trouble going to the bathroom, but it let me back up a little bit. At Golden, I would accidentally do a #3 in the bathroom sometimes. If you remember, let me explain again. In the accident, the connection from my brain to my eyes was partially severed. Now, I have very poor peripheral vision and depth perception. This often made it difficult for me to sit in the correct spot while pooping. Occasionally, I would go to sit and poop, and instead of pooping into the bowl I would poop onto the side of the seat; thus, my therapist, nurses, and parents coined the term taking a number 3. This happened a few times at Golden, where the nurses had the 'duty' to clean up the messes the patients made, including 'duty,' except, this time my mom had to do the duty. I'm sorry mom. Probably the worst job my parents had when I first got home was that every night, at some point throughout sleep, I would call my parents to help me fix my blankets when I got cold. Again, this time, it was a job for the nurses at Golden, now it was my parents' undertaking. It was annoying and not a great time for them, but they love me enough to take this all on. They surely were not going to stop now. As far as my recovery was concerned, and now that my left wrist could be worked on, I went to a different therapy in Westminster to focus mostly on my wrist and my hip a little too. The time frame of all this when I got home was a little bit blurry, but I spent most of my time watching TV, crying a lot, eating, sleeping, and calling Brady daily. Occasionally, I would have a friend visit me, sometimes Flutie, maybe once or twice a week. I had little control over my emotions at this point. After a lot of questioning God, why would He let this happen, and why didn't He just let me die. If I even believed anymore as I quickly lost my faith.

I think because I finally had time to be by myself for the first time since the accident to explore my feelings and what I had done to myself by having this accident. I think I may have cried enough for the rest of my life. My daily routine was as follows: wake up, watch TV for hours, cry for a while, fight through suicidal thoughts, and decide I couldn't do that to my family, every single day, no matter how much I wanted to. Then, learn some basic things on YouTube, or at least try, maybe work on a puzzle, eat some more food, perhaps shower, and then do the same thing again. When I would consider suicide, I would call my friend Tony to talk me down. These thoughts came a lot.

His dad committed suicide, and he saw firsthand the effects of the people left behind. Mitch took me to a neurologist, who talked to me about ways to deal with my injury, emotions, new life, and sadness. The most important thing that this doctor told me was that alcohol was very bad for me after my injury. If I needed something to calm my mind, cannabis is the better answer. This doctor also gave me a book called "When Bad Things Happen to Good People." This helped too. It explained that things just happen; whether you're a good person doesn't matter. This book helped a little as I always thought I was a good person, but I made some mistakes throughout my life, especially with girls. This book made me realize that being a good person didn't prevent me from having this accident. It could have saved me from something worse. There was no way to know. Though I was not thinking this way yet. The bad times are different for everyone, regardless of their situation. I didn't believe in God anymore. I always considered myself a Christian—a very lukewarm Christian but now I was no longer sure. I remember talking to my therapists at Golden about this very thing before I left, and they said, "I would think that the fact you lived through this experience and didn't die would make you believe more." I didn't see the big picture at all. It would have been abundantly clear if I had been more knowledgeable and had sincere faith. It wasn't. Instead, I cursed God for letting this happen to me. If God truly loved me, why would he let this happen to me. I was naïve and lacked understanding.

There was a girl I met at Golden who was doing her internship for school; her name is Ivy, and she is very attractive. Naturally, I would always flirt with her throughout our many conversations. I got to know her and how strong she was in her faith. She's a firm Christian and the last time I saw her before I left Golden, she invited me to go to her church with her. I went to church with her and hung out at her home, where I met her sweet mom and sister. I was confused about my faith after the accident, but going to church with her and talking with Uncle Billy helped me, though I still didn't feel anything. I was very attracted to her and enjoyed her company so I kept going. I have this very strong memory, I went to church with her and ended up crying my eyes out with a friend I met there. I couldn't control my strong emotions on this worship night at Crossroads Church in Westminster, MD. The next night of church, Mitch and my little brother Devin were arguing before the night service, and it became heated. I guess it was the first time I experienced extreme stress after the TBI, and my brain couldn't handle it.

I had a seizure, the worst one I can remember. An ambulance was called, and I stayed in the hospital for one whole week. Ivy visited me one day, which was nice, and Flutie also visited. That was the last time I went to that church, not on purpose. It just happened that way. Interesting. This is the moment I realized that seizure medicine only prevents seizures; it can't stop them completely. Ivy was my first kiss after Golden, and I liked her a lot. She's just such a great person. In time, though, we grew apart as she tried to start her life. I could tell I would not be a part of that, which was OK.

I realized I needed to start learning things independently; for instance, I could not clothe myself. Brady gave me the idea to start learning how to put on my socks by watching some "YouTube University." I took his advice and started watching videos on how to put them on. I know such a simple thing to learn, but it was not easy at all for me. I pushed myself and practiced for a whole day. By the end of the day I was very close; I could put on my right sock, and I decided that tomorrow I would learn the left. As I explained, my left side was partially paralyzed when I came out of the coma. This was going to be the most challenging part of the process. The next day, I could put my socks on my own for the first time since I had to restart my life completely, and gosh, was it a rush! I was so proud of myself, and I finally felt this for the first time since I came home. I felt so great after learning this; I didn't want to stop. I was excited to learn how to put on my clothes on my own. The next stop was my underwear; this one took a little more effort and concentration. I think because it was confusing to me. The most confusing part for me was that I had to understand that I had to put them on backward because I didn't have enough balance yet to do it standing. I had to put them on, always sitting down. Again, this was another two-day ordeal to get my underpants on correctly. I eventually got it done with some patience, which has never been my specialty, with multiple breaks throughout and a nap or two. As Cory would say, patience is a 'fruit chew instead' of a virtue. I decided to learn from bottom to top; it made sense to me that way. Once I got my socks and underwear figured out for the first time, I was ready to try on my shorts. I was confident about it because it's similar to putting on underwear; I got it quickly. I had trouble putting on my underwear and socks from time to time, but the more I did it, the better I got like anything. This lesson has followed me even today. To do everything I learned or learned again I must practice over and over until it becomes routine to do it correctly without having to think much, just like when I learned how to play the guitar. Eventually, it became unconscious, like how most people usually put their clothes on without thinking about it. Most of us, as brain injury survivors must be conscious and aware of every single second of life. At least, this is how it is for me. I realized this very recently. Let me not get ahead of myself.

All the showers in my house were bathtub showers, but I had problems lifting my legs and my balance the first year or so. So, I would always shower in my parents' shower, which was a walk-in shower. Since the accident, I have been stuck in this fear of falling in the shower, with poor balance and a lack of trust in my legs, which I still struggle with today. Though I have made leaps and bounds with that as time passed I had no trouble washing myself in the shower; I learned how to do that at Golden with Rhonda.

The next challenge for me at this juncture was to learn to put on my shirt correctly; again, it took me multiple days. Still, to this day, occasionally, I will put it on backward, usually when I am rushed or trying to put the shirt on in the car. Speaking of being rushed, I am awful at being rushed. I get very flustered, ending up taking even more time.

For the first few years post-accident, I was in constant cold, no matter the temperature outside or in the house. Most times, I would almost always have a sweatshirt on. Of course, I learned how to put on a sweatshirt like a shirt. The most challenging thing for me to put on, as far as clothes are concerned, has always been jeans or long pants. I guess because there is much more cloth to deal with and since I don't have great control over my legs, especially my left. Probably around this same time, Flutie had a new girlfriend who was very friendly, and sometimes he would bring her to my house to visit, which was always cool.

Occasionally, when it was nice outside, I would walk or try to run with the dogs. Of course, I couldn't run, but I thought, "Why not try since I have loved running my whole life?" Not to mention the challenge the dogs posed to me. We had four dogs almost always and a large fenced-in yard for them to frolic and run. My mom is kind of like a crazy cat lady, but instead of cats, dogs, and I have always loved dogs. My mom worked at a dog shelter for years and occasionally would come home with a dog, sometimes to keep or sometimes to shelter for a few days or weeks. That was my whole life; I loved being with the dogs every day and every night again, like before.

A neurologist told me that a good hobby for me post-TBI was to start doing puzzles to exercise my brain and left hand. After my left hand/wrist surgery, I went to do some occupational therapy OT to work on my left hand. I could hardly use it consciously because my brain was not connected to it anymore. I could barely use it for a long time, even though I had some excellent therapy for it. This therapy worked with my left wrist and right hip, including some time spent on the stairs.

At some point during my first few months home again, my parents took me to the Johns Hopkins Wilmer Eye Institute in Baltimore to see what was going on with my vision because, before the accident, I had perfect 20/20 vision. Those days are gone now. At Wilmer, the doctors and neuro-optometrist (an eye doctor specializing in brain and eye connection) did a few tests at this appointment, and they came back with the diagnosis that nothing could be done. The connections from my eyes to my brain were damaged, causing all my vision problems. Neither glasses nor contacts can fix this vision impairment. I knew before I went that my peripheral vision and depth perception were imperfect now, but I knew what had happened and what had caused this. I learned that my vision went from 20/20 to something like 20/15 or something like this. Don't quote me on this; it's been a long time, but my vision has significantly worsened since the fall. I think the biggest problem with those tests was that I was not able to concentrate so soon after the accident. I have trouble with concentration now, more than five years after this injury. Within the first year of living at home again, my parents, mostly Mitch, realized that I could not control my emotions.

18

God Uses Our Challenges for

Good

I forgot to mention this, but the first trip I took after coming home from Golden was to Uncle Billy's house for that Christmas because Uncle Billy hosted Christmas every year at his house. Once I could go and celebrate Christmas with the whole family, boy was I excited. Not only did I leave and go to a different place for the first time since my life drastically changed, but also because I was so happy to see extended family too! It was a great trip, and I stayed for one whole week. While my family went for the Christmas celebration, only I stayed for the entire week. I always loved spending time with Uncle Billy and his family; this was no exception. It's kind of crazy to think about now, but this week with their family helped my closest cousin, Garrett decide to go to college to be a PT/OT. He graduated and works in that field today.

It was an excellent trip for me and helped Garrett create his life plan because of my crazy situation. He helped me all week. This was a great first trip for me. I mean, before I would go to their house often. I wanted to continue this trend as long as possible, and I did with my whole family for Christmas and then one more week. As spring came, I continued my wrist therapy and OT, with stairs mixed in. One day, after I had been home for a few months my aunt Heather visited us and stayed for a day or two. I was not great with my body and abilities yet, always trying but skittish because I didn't trust myself, especially my legs. Heather, my mom's half-sister, somehow realized I could do more than I was showing because of my fears. After some conversation with Mitch, he and Heather were arguing with me, and he was trying to push me to try different things. I was always skittish because I didn't trust myself, especially my legs. Heather, my mom's half-sister, somehow realized I could do much more than I was showing because of my fears. After some conversation with Mitch, he and Heather were arguing with me, and he was trying to push me to try to take a shower in the shower upstairs in the tub shower. The conversation became heated because I had become comfortable showering in my parents' room. He wanted me to try showering upstairs for the first time. My aunt was a little bit nervous, but against all odds I went up the stairs and took my first shower in a shower with a tub since the accident. Gosh, I felt like a champion upon completion, and I thanked Mitch for showing me the tough love that pushed me to even try. Throughout this process, Mitch always pushed me to try things I didn't have the confidence to try on my own for the first time. For example, when I went home from Golden, he left the wheelchair on the sidewalk. This time was a different situation, but the same push. Sometimes, I need that little push. I never needed this much before, but this is an entirely new me now. I had a lot more complications than I had ever experienced before. This is where my frustration came from. Since I was born, things have been kind of easy for me—everything from school and studying to pushing myself for sports. I was not a natural, but I was good enough at pushing myself and training myself to be athletic.

There's no training to prepare yourself for everything that comes with a TBI. It's all uncharted territory. I mean, most people don't plan on getting a TBI in their lifetime. That's just life. You must adjust to anything that comes your way. For me, this was completely restarting my life. I did not want it, but life gave me no choice. You may be thinking, man this dude has a great attitude. During this exact time back then, my attitude was not good at all.

I was so confused, depressed, and angry about this whole situation that I created for myself, not on purpose, but it didn't matter. I was here, and I could have very easily avoided it. No one ever thinks hiking alone would have horrendous consequences, but it happened to me. This was an athletic, strong, and confident dude. I struggled with why for a couple of months, maybe even year. I had read this book, but my thoughts still raced. Was it some kind of karma for the bad way I treated women in my early 20s? I always try to be a good person, a kind person. What did I do in my life to be like this?

How will I ever find happiness again? Not to mention a girl who could deal with my extreme difficulties. I had this same conversation for years weekly with my best friends and Brady. Are my days of being with a girl gone forever now? My friends had no answer to that question, but they always told me to stay motivated and keep pushing. I had no choice but to do so. I guess because girls were always a large part of my life before. It was easygoing, but not anymore. Certainly, I should not have thought about that. I had much more important things to worry about, but my mind always raced. When I was not wallowing in self-pity, crying, or doing small things to improve my injuries, like trying to write again, working on puzzles, or napping. I was watching TV and trying to put on clothes with ease. Before I knew it, it was the prelude to summer. It was a beautiful, almost summer day. Mitch was working on cleaning out the pool before he filled it for the summer. The sun was bright with not a cloud in the sky. I wanted to go and speak with him and give him company as he worked on the pool, but to do so I had to walk down the deck stairs with no railing.

At this point, I was not great with stairs, and I didn't trust myself to walk them without a railing. I was afraid to try without help. I was furious because I had no way to get down the stairs to talk with him. A few minutes passed, fighting against my emotions, knowing that I was too scared to walk down the stairs on my own without a railing, and it made me furious. Then, out of nowhere, I picked up a large, heavy flowerpot and threw it at Mitch. It was at this moment that Mitch realized that I needed help maybe some therapy or a psychiatrist to figure out what was going on inside my mind. God knows I didn't want to be throwing things at Mitch. I started some therapy with a cool dude who was once in a band himself. I also got some depression medicine too. I had some powerful thoughts of suicide fighting me at least once a day. I knew I could never do it because my parents, family, and friends went through so much for me to live. I learned how selfish it would be. I just couldn't. It didn't keep my mind from racing with very dark thoughts, not to mention all the people I would leave behind. I had friend, Tony who experienced his dad taking his own life and he always talked me through these thoughts and emotions and put me back in a better state of mind. He always helped a lot. I began therapy in Westminster.

This was my first time going to a mental therapy post-Golden. I knew I needed help with my emotions. I was prescribed some antidepressant or mood medication, and it helped. Well, I'm unsure if that was the reason, the therapy, or maybe both. I think it was around the same time that my younger brother invited me to smoke weed with him. This was my first-time smoking since the day before I had the accident. I didn't know what to expect with my new brain, but I loved it. It finally relaxed my mind from all the stress, feelings, and thoughts plaguing me for years. It didn't fix any problems but it gave me some much-needed solace and rest. I think I could relax my mind for the first time since my life changed completely. For the next two years, I smoked almost every day to rest my mind from those awful feelings, emotions, and reflections for a few hours, smoking way too much and far too often.

Some people might not agree with this choice, but it helped me throughout this long journey. Until this first-time smoking, during the most difficult of days where I wished I would have died from the fall five stories down, it kept me on an even keel and helped to keep my emotions from getting the best of me. I must say, before this horrific injury, I just smoked it for fun, but I had a new appreciation for it now. They say the brain is not yet done growing until age 25, and since I've always been a huge health freak, I never started smoking it regularly until after this accident. I had already turned 25 during my coma. It's funny looking back because my long-term memory was bad before I fell. Now, my long-term memory is great. Only my short-term memory was affected. Once I realized that smoking was not too bad but could be beneficial to the neuroplasticity of a damaged brain, I largely overdid it. I would smoke every single night with Zauhn and sometimes his lady friend. She was also very cool. For those who don't know, neuroplasticity is the brain's ability to create new pathways in the brain for ones that were damaged. Looking back, I wish I had never started again. Was I addicted? That's a good question. I think mentally, I was for sure for many years. It made my day different and calmed my mind at first. I also realized that it made me much lazier and made music a different experience. I mean, if I were high, I could experience every little background sound of each song, and I would not be able to realize I had not smoked or searched for it. This played a role in my recovery process in terms of my moods, thoughts, and just a better feeling about my life going forward. It did make me lazy. Somehow, Mitch got his hands on a nice Bow flex machine we kept in the outside garage. It was great for me to work out a little bit without too much help. A few friends would occasionally take me to the same gym I went to before. It was awesome because I was friends with the manager too.

These friends would take me, but they were living their own lives too. Eventually, they stopped having time, which I don't fault them for. This Bow flex was awesome for me, especially when I had no more chance to go to the gym with my friends. The coolest thing was all these awesome friends who came to spend time with me when I got home, friends I hadn't spent time with since high school. It was great; I was always their friend in high school, but after we went our separate ways, they returned to spend time with me when I needed it. It made me feel great that after all this time, they heard about my difficulties and wanted to share some love.

By this time, it was summer Uncle Billy and his family invited me and his oldest son's fiancée to go to Deep Creek Lake in western Maryland for vacation. Uncle Billy's family consisted of Harrison, the oldest son, Garrett, and one daughter, the youngest named Elyse, and Aunt Kim. I have always been very close with all of them. I was super excited to go, especially with the soon-to-be new family member. This was the first time I stopped smoking cannabis since I started again, and it was fine, which made me feel good. Deep Creek Lake is a huge lake where you can swim, ride boats, and jet ski. We did all of that, as there's much to do on and off the water. I practiced swimming before I left and realized I could still swim, but not nearly as well as before. Being cautious, the first time I went into the water on this trip, I wore a life jacket just in case. I quickly learned I could swim well enough not to need the life jacket. It made me feel like an adult.

I think I was there for one week, spending great time with them, conversing, learning, and getting to know Harrison's fiancé. Her name is Taylor, and I got to know her very well on this trip. I realized that I love her too. She is a very great addition to the family. We did many fun things there: exploring the town, trying to play tennis, going to a new church, going to a farmers' market, going to a small museum, and conquering many stairs. The house we stayed in had so many stairs to go anywhere in the house, but I overcame them, becoming known as "Stairsman." I think I got so much better at stairs by doing them when I started smoking with my brother because I would have to walk up and down the stairs to go up and smoke. It is fascinating that, after the accident I would get very different effects from cannabis, sometimes affecting my balance and coordination a lot. I would need to focus well while walking the stairs, especially if I were high. It was okay because I always enjoyed the challenge, especially if I was immediately rewarded. On the trip, we read a Christian book, learning about how God uses our lives and difficulties for good. I was just not ready to accept it yet. I had deep conversations with all the family members, including Taylor, about everything, always thinking about what was waiting for me in the future, what to do now, and how I could find love, among many other things. Man, I ate great on this trip, enjoying fantastic different foods. It was a great change of pace, and I enjoyed it 1000%. I bunked with Garrett, who was always there for me when I needed help, preparing him for his future career. It was a much-needed change for me and fun to break from my routine. Upon returning home, I was excited to continue my therapy, work out again, and smoke too much again.

19

The Hard
Part

Occasionally, friends like Flutie, Zauhn, or Tony would come over and chill with me. Every night I was available, Zauhn would come over to smoke with me, and I loved that time with him. I could talk deeply with one of my closest friends as I was trying to get past a lot of difficult emotions and physical challenges. Brady called me every day too for the first five years which certainly helped. I needed that. We talked about everything, especially how I could ever find a girlfriend again. I had the same conversation with all my friends. It was not a significant concern at this point, but I always had it in my mind, especially after Abby returned to her own life. I mean, this was only a year and a half or two years after my accident. I had made giant strides during this time, mentally as well as physically, but I was not where I wanted to be. The hardest part for me was patience; I struggled with this throughout my life. There's no quick fix for a brain injury. I quickly realized it would take time, patience, and hard work. Each day posed its challenges, probably for the first two or so years with the emotional hurdles that plagued me the most, including confusion, anxiety, depression, and fear of the unknown regarding my future and my dream of being a father or husband one day. I felt that that dream was pretty much gone now. These thoughts would come and go each day. When the thoughts and feelings were too strong, I would try to push them away by smoking cannabis, working out, or sometimes both. When I left Golden, I never realized that the hard part was just beginning.

It was easy there because I had nothing but therapies to keep my mind occupied but now, I had to rediscover myself. A new self I didn't want, where nothing will be easy again. It was precisely the opposite of my life before. I always loved pushing myself to the limit, but it was much more difficult with my new brain. Most of my personality was still intact, but I could not say the same about my intelligence, body, and mind. First off, I no longer had complete control of my body movements and my tongue. I could no longer think quickly, making me much less witty, as my tongue and brain were not significantly connected like before. It's petty to complain because I am alive which is more than most doctors had imagined. Indeed, no doctor thought that I would ever walk again. Still, sometimes it upsets me all the things I can no longer do that I love. But hindsight is 20-20, as they say. I'm not sure who "they" are, but I trust them. I don't know how everyone else deals with their brain injuries, their difficulties, their progress, and their time frames. This is my experience. If I didn't have such a great support system, my friends and family, it would have been far more challenging and who knows if I would have ever been where I am today. For instance, if I never had Zauhn and my little brother to smoke with every day for years and Brady to call every day to talk through my depression and fears, plus my other friends (especially Tony), to keep me from succumbing to the bad thoughts in my mind that fought me daily, who knows where I would be today, as every day I would feel that I wish I would have died from the accident or I wanted to end my life myself.

I never had too much trouble with motivation, especially at the start. Still, as I started to move on to more complex tasks that were easy before, it became more challenging with the memories of how easy they were to do in the past. I knew I needed to keep pushing on, and things would get easier in time, but again, the thoughts in my mind came and disrupted my progress. Usually, it was only for a short time until I smoked, took a break, or both. Then, my focus would return. This was my life for a reasonable amount of time, with some fun activities in between, including the wedding of a longtime family friend whose younger brother was a great friend of mine, and Brady was a friend of his brother.

At this wedding, I got too drunk on wine, and then someone offered me some marijuana, too. I smoked with the wine in my system, and it was all over. I had gotten drunk before this time with my new brain, but this was the first and last time I smoked with alcohol. I very quickly lost complete control of my balance and focus. I had to have a friend and Mitch carry me to the car. I learned my lesson about smoking and drinking at the same time. I thought, "Why not drink a little bit?" It was a special occasion. I know that the neurologist suggested that I don't drink anything stronger than beer anymore, and wine was a bad choice. I drank a lot of Red's Apple Ale at the golf tournament, which was also a special occasion. So, I drank on this particular occasion too.

The drunkest I got since the accident was one night Tony invited me to go to a bar with him, and it was the first time for me to go to a bar since I was with Brady and Eric in CA. I was excited to spend time with Tony and get out in public. Tony and I proceeded to drink Cosmos until I again lost complete control of my balance. It was funny because Mitch and Tony had to carry me into my bed. Tony said the last thing Mitch said before we left was don't have too much fun, and we did. This was the last time I drank heavily for many years. I could tell my brain didn't love it, so I tried to prevent it from happening again. Aside from this learning situation, Tony helped me so much through my extreme post-golden depression. It was so strong I considered ending the pain and hardship daily. Luckily, I was consoled continually by Tony, who lost his father to the same thing. He would always tell me, "It's not worth it," and I listened to him each time.

Abby invited me and Shane to the Science Center in Baltimore one weekend. It was a great adventure as well. I don't exactly remember what took place, but Abby always wanted to take me places to get out into the public and ensure I continued living my life. I remember one time she also took me to the pumpkin patch. We had a lot of fun there, made memories, and took pictures. My next adventure was going to Nick, the drummer of the band's wedding, with Abby as my date. She took me shopping for my outfit, and we were both excited. It was almost like, I mean, Abby and my first actual date. I was excited but also a little bit nervous. I was not great at buttoning my pants, not to mention with a belt. I knew now after this time, that really, my whole life most things did not embarrass me. Lucky for me, especially now because I was continuously doing embarrassing things, not by choice usually. I was never close to Nick's wife but always happy for them both. This would be a good chance to be around many people, some of whom I know and others I don't. Don't tell Nick this, but I don't remember a lot of the details of the night, and I wasn't even drinking. I do remember that it was fun. We danced, ate, and enjoyed ourselves with the old band members. The strongest memory I have of this whole night is that, at some point, I had to go and pee, and I needed to have Abby help me with the belt because some people at the wedding didn't know my situation. They thought for some reason that Abby and I were going to the bathroom together to have sex. Which we were not. The furthest that we ever went after the accident was kissing.

After Nick's wedding, Abby and I started growing distant as the days passed; it was no one's fault. Abby had to start her own life and I had to start picking up the pieces of mine. Not to mention how far she lived from me—at least an hour and a half each way. She was great and was there for me, I cannot thank her enough for all she did for me. I'll never forget that. I saw her one more time before we lost touch. Again, at a wedding, this time for Flutie's neighbor in Baltimore City. A friend from high school and college that I also knew. A great guy who was close friends with Flutie, so I was invited to the wedding Abby too because she is or was good friends with the girl who is getting married to him.

I was not going with Abby as my date this time, which was OK. I was confused about why she didn't want to go with me. The more I thought about it, the more apparent it became that she wanted to go and have more fun without taking care of me. At this moment, I understood that she was young and wanted to experience life without having someone hold her back. Slowly but surely, she became further away from me, but I never took it personally. I came to terms with it and continued through this arduous journey I was on.

By this point, I had gotten on disability through the hard work of Mitch, and he got me into a program that was to help find me a job. This program, which I guess was to get people off disability. I did not have the skills yet to have a job at all, but I still tried. This program gave me some tests to test my work skills, and after many tests the director concluded that there was a slight chance I could get a job as a transporter at the local hospital. If there was a chance, I was like, I would try. I went through all the screening processes, including a drug test. Mitch and I tried one of these body-flushing kits to help cheat the drug test. I thought I could not work a job where I couldn't smoke at this point. We tried, and I went to this drug test where I peed in a cup, a challenge for me and my poor vision. A day or two went by, and I got the call that I failed the drug test. This program had ceased for me.

I thought I would be done with trying to find a

job and instead focus on myself. I continued to work out daily, did exercises to strengthen my left hand, and tried to work on walking slowly and quickly and controlling my emotions. It was a far cry from the 4-minute mile I was used to, but I had to start somewhere. Nick's wedding was in November of 2016, which I think was before I even got home from Golden. The next few weddings I went to were after I had already gotten home. Since I never wanted to stop playing and recording music with my friends, I had one song I was very close to finishing before my accident happened. I decided to finish it with the help of Eric, Paul, and a local producer I worked with. This song would come to be known as "Let You Go," the one song I worked on and recorded after the fall off the cliff. It is not my favorite or the best song I have done, but it was the first opportunity to try singing and making a song with my new brain. I only did the vocals, and I was proud of it. Eric did the drums and the lead guitar; Paul did the bass; and he helped with a lot with the entire process with the producer Kenny, the same producer that we used to record the Friends cover with the band Danger Parker and the song "All the Miles" before the accident.

After we finished that song, my life was unchanged for a time. I slowly improved on many things, especially walking these stairs up and down. I did walk down to the basement as it became colder outside to work on some walking. Since I was 13, I was always afraid to get fat and look like John. That's why I wanted to work out until I realized it would improve my athletic performance. More than that though, I was always afraid to get fat. I quickly became addicted to working out and the endorphins that come with it. After the accident though, I kind of lost my ability to push myself with cardio. This, combined with the doctor at Golden explaining to me that I needed to eat as much as I could help my brain heal, made me much fatter than I wanted and I didn't like looking at myself. It made me feel kind of gross and ugly. I mean, it was still kind of early in my recovery process but I wanted to feel better about myself, my body, my brain, and my life. I told myself that no matter what I would find a way to get my body back. As time passed, I started to update my friends and family with my everyday struggles and progress through Facebook Live to make a little vlog. This was good for me and everyone who wanted to know what my day was like after the huge, life-altering experience I had to go through to learn to live again. I kind of thought to myself, "What is a way I can use my experiences to help others going through their hard times?"

I wanted to find a way to help others through their awful and difficult times and show others that there's always a way. I started making little vlogs. I recorded about ten or so, and then I decided to work on writing a book about my whole life, but I could not type at this juncture. I'm still very slow now. In Maryland, a friend from high school said she would help with my typing for this book, but her life got in the way. So, I asked someone else who is a very smart man and was a great friend of Brady and mine alike. Then, the same thing happened over time, with life getting in the way. It was OK again. As the months went on, I would just type on my phone or speak with talk-to-text notes on my phone. My entire life, I always dreamed of somehow being remembered. First, I thought it would be through football, then music. Now, I thought it could somehow be through my life story.

Not to mention how much I could help others who go through the painful process of fighting a TBI or any trauma or arduous and persistent struggle; just like with my journey, I had a plan for my life—to find a way to be remembered. I found a way to pursue this through my everyday battles unceremoniously. I will continue to press through every day for my remaining days. Regardless of what you are going through at this point in your life, it may not be a brain injury or anything quite as severe or more. Know that there's always hope. If this book and story could inspire you to oppose this altercation head-on, I will die happy knowing I inspired anyone and was remembered in a way that helps others through their misadventures. All the problems and difficulties experienced in life can be beaten or at least challenged with enough willpower and a strong support system. Just keep reading...

20

Going South, in a Good Way

I always knew I had a great support system, but I only realized how much it helped once I spoke with survivors of TBIs who didn't have a great support system. Gosh, it makes a world of difference. Thank you so much to all my friends and family who were there for me throughout the toughest times, especially Flutie. The months and seasons continued, and the following winter came and went. We played in the snow, I had recorded one song and started this book with notes on my phone. Before I knew it, it was spring again. I was still working out, and I started walking or strolling on the treadmill as I tried to get back into better shape. We had a huge house in Hampstead, and now that Mitch could no longer work because of his heart disease, we really couldn't afford this large house and all the amenities that came with it. Not to mention losing all their savings for my sake. While I was busy smoking cannabis, Mitch and my mom were busy trying to find a different place to move, both cheaper and more southern. After much searching, they decided on Cape Coral, Florida. About 18 hours south from my hometown in Hampstead. It was kind of bittersweet knowing that I would be leaving my comfort zone and friends. Still, I think I knew this would be a good change for me because I wouldn't have to deal with the cold winter anymore, which is much more difficult to deal with now that I am always cold.

That wasn't the main reason for the move, but I was very gracious regardless. I mean, my family knew how cold I always was, and in this new place, it very rarely gets cold. I was excited to try different therapies and make some new friends. I knew I could try Tinder there too. I had never tried using Tinder since my new life started. What was the point? I know what girls in my age range are like in their early to late 20s. They are looking for a guy who can support them. That was not me. Not to mention, I was busy trying to take care of myself and learning the small things I needed to learn to be an adult once again. However, this would all change when I finally moved to Florida. My parents' friends and some of Shane's friends helped a lot with the moving process and trying to sell a lot of stuff. We could not take to our new home, including a pool table, which was the heaviest thing. We needed many of Shane's friends to come and help move it. Then, my parents decided to put on a garage sale to get rid of some stuff and make money for the move. All the while, I was saying goodbye to my friends a lot of whom completely lost touch with me after my accident or started their families which is awesome. My close friends stayed around me or kept in touch with me through the phone or FaceTime, like talking to Brady almost daily. After we did the yard sale, cleaned our house, and packed everything we would take. Mitch rented a U-Haul, packed up all four dogs, and we were on our way. In the heat of summer.

I remember Devin driving his car with a couple of dogs; my mom and I rode in our SUV, and I think Shane rode with Mitch in the U-Haul with at least one dog. The drive to Cape Coral, Florida, was not a short one. It took about 18 hours, and we split it into two days. The coolest part about the drive was that we got to stop occasionally for the dogs to pee or for us to pee. We were excited, especially Devin, because he would be attending school there once we settled. Devin had some pull from his excellent lacrosse skills in high school. Devin has always been great at all sports involving a ball. He was a great athlete in high school, with lacrosse being his best sport. He got invited to come and play at Flagler College in Florida, which was far from where we moved but he had a car and jumped at the opportunity to play lacrosse at this school. It is interesting, but my parents had never seen this house except in pictures; it would be somewhat of a surprise for all of us when we arrived. Nothing very crazy happened on the drive, but we were all very excited to see our new home. After driving for 18 hours and stopping to sleep once, we finally arrived in Cape Coral, Florida.

The next challenge was to unpack everything from the U-Haul. Our furniture, our beds, TVs, and every other thing we had that was large. Not too much, but not too easy. We got through it. My parents came to Florida with very little money too. The first thing we did when we arrived after the day of unpacking was go to a small local restaurant, and Shane immediately asked for a job application. For the next many years, he worked at this restaurant. Somewhere along the line of the first month, we were there I drank a 6-pack of Redd's Apple Ale, causing a seizure and an excruciating migraine accompanying it. The first seizure since the one I was hospitalized for. I took this as a sign not to drink anymore, and I still to this day don't.

As time passed, Mitch got me into some new physical therapy so I could learn to walk without sliding my feet and work on my balance and some more OT to help me work on my left hand and learn how to use it. Lastly, I still needed more speech therapy. All the therapies, minus my physical, were not far from our home which was nice, but the physical one was 30 or 40 minutes away. Beggars can't be choosers, and I think I was a beggar at this point. For the next maybe year, I was going to therapy at least twice or three times a week with my parents driving. I also continued my cannabis bingeing most days and exercising at home as much as I could manage, with no money to spend on a gym membership. Little did I know that my life and world were about to change.

Every day, I would wake up, eat breakfast, maybe smoke, depending on my schedule that day, then nap.

Then work out, depending on my therapy schedule. If I had no therapy that day or in the morning, I would not smoke until after therapy. At this stage, I thought I needed to smoke because my moods would start to control me, but once I smoked my emotions would be controlled once again. Brady would always say that when I felt like I needed to smoke, it was time for an attitude adjustment with smoking. That's what I thought at least. At this point, I started exploring what Tinder offered in my area. I thought long and hard about my profile and whether I should start with my accident, using the article from Maryland explaining it. Or if I should keep that secret. The thought I had was that I would not want to waste people's time. I would start with my story, and if she didn't want to deal with this whole situation, she could take a pass on me. Most girls would usually stop talking to me when they heard that I couldn't drive. Most girls trying to find a guy on Tinder in the Cape Coral area didn't want a guy who couldn't drive. I guess all my other problems, too. Not to mention that all the girls I found on Tinder lived far away, which was not great because I couldn't drive. I met some girls on this app we matched, but the same thing always happened: the girl would read my story from the newspaper in Maryland, feel compassion, talk a little, and then quickly disappear.

When I was at Golden, I was interviewed for a newspaper article telling my story. Thank God because it was huge for me to share my story with others, especially girls on Tinder. If you like, you can find this article on Google; look up "Cody Ridenour Hiking Accident." They would talk to me for a week, maybe two, then stop talking to me altogether. I could not blame them; I came with a lot of baggage. The girl would say, "Oh man, you're like a miracle. I'm so sorry you had to go through that." Then they would ghost me. Brady gave me some tips, and Nick Strong suggested I try some other apps, like Hinge and Bumble. I did not do well on Hinge. Against all odds, I finally met one girl on Bumble, and we planned that she would come to my house and eat some pizza. We planned this pizza night for a week, and then she stopped answering me the day before. I was bummed, but it wasn't a huge deal. I had no real confidence that I would find a mate anymore, especially after this colossal life accident. I kind of continued looking at Tinder from time to time, just to pass the time. Without ever really having the real thought that I could ever find a girl to date me with all my difficulties. I wish I could say I never lost hope, but I did.

Not long after I lost hope, Zauhn hooked me up with a friend he met through his college football teammate who was from my new area in Cape Coral/Fort Myers FL, as a way for us to buy weed. I don't remember this guy at all, but I met a nice girl who lived much further away from my home through buying weed. She and I became friends. One day, she drove 30 or 40 minutes to pick me up and take me around the city. I couldn't walk for long at this time, but I had a good time with her. She was pretty, but I was not ready to get intimate with any girls yet. I wanted to kiss her but couldn't find the confidence to do it. I don't think I believed in myself enough to put someone in my complicated life with all the terrible problems that would come with it. She is such a nice person and I felt bad putting her in that position. If we got close, she would have to take care of me. It wasn't fair, especially since she was in college. To an extent, I felt like I was saving her from the hard life she would get pulled into if I got her to fall for me. Through this meeting with a girl, the first one in Florida, I realized I could not put myself out there to meet girls yet. Regardless, I continued to spend time on Tinder from time to time just to pass the time and look at some pretty girls.

Then came the coronavirus pandemic, which officially started on March 11, 2020.

As a result of this, everything shut down. Interestingly, not long before the virus came, I was told by my physical therapists that there was not much more they could do for me. (Sound familiar?) To this day, I don't believe that. Regardless, around the time the virus came, I had run out of therapy appointments that my insurance would cover until the following year. I had to stop therapy for the year, which was OK because the virus came anyway. All the medical buildings were closed for the whole year. Depending on where you were living, most things were shut down. I tried my luck on Tinder and would do home workouts every day, usually following the "athleteX.com" videos on YouTube. I did as much as I could with my difficulties with my wrist and trying to control my body. I would walk Rocco our small Boston terrier, at least twice or thrice daily. I enjoyed it. Our other dogs are large dogs, and it is harder for me to control for a walk. This was the first time our dogs ever had to be walked. They had a large, fenced area to run around the rest of their lives. This new home in Florida had no fence, at least not yet. I tried to continue some therapy at home; I did what I could while the virus was taking control of the country. I continued watching TV, watching a lot of Impractical Jokers, and working on this book and my body just in case I ever met a girl. I'll be ready with abs. I talked to a few girls on Tinder but nothing exciting. Then, one day I matched with the most beautiful light brown girl. I had no choice but to speak with her.

21

The Girl

This gorgeous girl was named Livia, like Olivia, but without the "O." It was a beautiful name and obviously not American, which first attracted me. I tried not to get too excited; this girl was clearly out of my league. As you have seen throughout this story, I never back down from a challenge. This was a different kind of challenge here, but I had to try by starting a conversation with the most beautiful girl I had matched with on Tinder yet. I had no idea if she would even answer, especially being the prettiest caramel skin beauty, with long brown hair and eyes like the light brown of a forest of trees of the Amazon. Maybe she would never answer like so many others before.

As luck would have it, she did respond to that first message after we matched. It was probably something along the lines of, "Damn, you are gorgeous; where are you from?" It became abundantly clear from my time on this application that most people in Cape Coral were not originally from here, just like me. She explained that she was from Brazil and had been here for a few months. I started to get very excited about talking to her more and more and learning about her. Then, out of nowhere, she stopped answering. Come on, not again. I thought this conversation was going well and I had high hopes. I guess it was too good to be true. It was back to searching again for the next girl to start a conversation with until I found myself in the same situation.

Regrettably, I worked on trying it all again. One fateful day, maybe a week later I was exploring the girls on Tinder again and by golly, it was Livia, the Brazilian beauty again. Without a second to spare, I gave her the like once more, painfully and anxiously waiting for the match. It could not have been more than a minute, maybe 30 seconds, and we were matched again. Thank God! I was back! I started the same way again, and she quickly remembered that we had talked once before. It was abundantly clear that I didn't remember. Luckily for me, though she remembered, I had a great idea of how to get past my not remembering. Since she had no information about me yet, I chose this moment to send her the article hoping my story would excuse me from not having memory of matching with her before. It worked. I did have a short-term memory problem after this accident. She proceeded to read the article about my accident, and she cried. Her crying reading my story before meeting me said a lot about her heart.

This was again very attractive to me; of all the people I have shared my story with on Tinder, this was the first one that said they cried. At this moment, I knew she could be the one I'd been waiting for more than four years.

We continued our conversation, I learned that she moved from Brazil by herself with a lifelong dream to experience different cultures and see other places not only America. I'm very grateful she chose America, mainly after seeing America on TV shows and movies. I also learned that she was a civil engineer in Brazil before she moved. Not only was she a great person with a great heart, not to mention freaking beautiful, but she was very intelligent too. I felt like I had won the jackpot. As the days went on, my routine continued with the bonus of messaging with Livia all day and all night. This was a huge step in her life because her dream in America was to improve her English and one day become so good that she sounded like a native speaker. The whole reason she got the app was that since the entire country was shut down from the virus, she was trying to improve her English. Her friend encouraged her to try downloading this app and talking to people. It worked, and I thanked God for her friend. In my profile on the app, I explained that I could not drive. I didn't explain everything about my problems, but that I smoked cannabis almost every day. Thankfully, that was not much of a concern for her with everything I went through to get to where I am now.

By this point, I would eat a lot of frozen dinners because I could use the microwave and make a PBJ and that was my diet, minus at least two bananas, one apple, and sometimes some snacks. Sometimes, a protein shake or protein bars. I was far too worried about getting fat again, so much that I would eat nothing past 7:30 PM. I would not get fat again. I got slightly too skinny, according to some friends and my parents. I would spend the whole day texting with Livia, and she always took care of her friend's baby while his parents were at work. This was a lifetime family friend of her family and her. She had moved from Brazil with her husband before Livia arrived. That's where she lived at the time, in a one-bedroom apartment sleeping on a mattress in the living room. It was not too bad for her to start. They had a baby when they moved to America and named him John. Livia became the nanny. Quickly though, she made her first large American purchase: a car. An SUV; it was blue and old but did the job for her. This was a huge deal in her eyes because there was no way she could ever afford a car in Brazil, and now she could have a way to get a job. She had another Brazilian friend who worked cleaning rental properties in the area on a small island, a huge vacation spot. Sanibel Island. This island was not very close, probably around 45 minutes without traffic. She would clean some rental properties in the morning and afternoon and then deliver food at night. This was her life at the start of her American adventure.

It was not too long until I realized how shy of a girl she was, though she was courageous enough to leave her home country for a new one on a 9-hour flight with no job and only one friend in the country. After some time, it was time for us to FaceTime or talk on the phone. She was too shy to FaceTime with me, so I talked her into talking to me on the phone. She was embarrassed to speak with me on the phone because of her English, which was not bad either. She had only been in the country for 4 or 5 months, so I understood. I appreciated her fear, and I shared with her that I was still going through speech therapy myself. So, 'don't be embarrassed speaking; I have troubles myself.' She didn't know me yet, but I would never make fun of someone, especially someone trying to learn something new. After this first phone call, it quickly became a nighttime routine for us to talk on the phone. Sometimes for hours, sometimes until very late, until I couldn't stay up any longer. As time passed, we connected and started to enjoy each other's company on the phone. We talked about meeting in person, but it was at the height of the pandemic, and Mitch, my dad has heart failure. I think I was more worried about him than he was. Mitch gave me the green light to invite her over. I wasted no time preparing for the evening. It was August 11th, 2020. She had to work in the morning and then came to my house. Pandemic be damned.

I did some research the entire day before she came over just in case it got to this point later in the day or night. I was trying to learn some stuff in Portuguese, her native language. Or, as Mitch calls it, Brazilian.

I tried to learn to say "I want to kiss you" in Portuguese. You know, just in case it went very well. I had high hopes. She arrived around four or five in the afternoon. I hugged her for the first time, and from the first moment I saw her in person, I knew I would marry her if given the chance. When I walked out of the house to welcome her and hug her for the first time, she saw my limp. I guess it never dawned on me to explain my walking difficulties to her. I had a very considerable limp at this point in my recovery, and I think that was the first thing that caught her eye. The first thing that caught my eye when I saw her in person was the radiance she unknowingly possessed. A kind of purity of soul. That, combined with the soft, flowing dark brown hair gently blowing in the wind as if it were a field of blackberry petunias, I immediately noticed her very fit, athletic body. I saw her on FaceTime, but seeing this perfect smile in person was very different. The next thing that confused her and blew her mind was immediately inviting her inside to meet my family. I never gave it a second thought. I just did it. I knew in the back of my mind that she would be a large part of my life for a long time. I always wanted to find a girl that my mom and family loved, especially my mom. That's why I immediately wanted her to meet my family. Mitch always stuck in my mind that family is the most important thing. He learned this from his dad. I'll always keep this in my heart and teach it to my kids. We decided to go to a local park in Cape Coral. It was nicknamed the manatee park; it was a nice park with cement cuts of manatees kissing, called Sirena Vista.

We did not go to a restaurant or any more traditional date spot due to the pandemic, but it was a nice and romantic date spot. We just walked around the small park and talked for the first time in person. I was already in love from the first sight of her, and I could see she enjoyed my personality and sense of humor. It was all great. After a few hours I decided to show her what I had learned in Portuguese. I tried to speak this sentence. I had practiced for two days: "I want to kiss you." I said everything correctly except the pronoun you, "você." For some reason, I pronounced "you" "Voce." I have no idea why, but I pronounced the word with a Ch instead of a C. Voche... Which is incorrect. It worked anyway. After we kissed with my poor kissing form, I was smitten. I thought she was a godsend for me.

I sincerely thought this was a girl God sent directly to me and that I still had a purpose on earth. She would help me get to where I must go to live this purpose to help others who have been through what I've been through or trauma. All the hard days, tears, pain, and scars. These were all things I had to go through to become the man I am and to help others who had been through something traumatic like I had. Maybe…

When you feel that there's no hope. I'm here to show you and tell you that no matter what you're fighting through, there is always hope; it's just a matter of finding it. I've had many conversations with friends and family, asking why God would let this happen to me. Why did He save me? How can I ever find happiness again after losing everything I loved in my life before? As I write this, I'm still going through the process of getting better and trying to get my life back together, but I have learned so much through this process. I think I've become a much better person, less selfish. I was drinking way too much and just not living the life I wanted, with no idea how to get where I wanted to be, so God took control. The most challenging part of this recovery process was/is finding the energy always to be aware of my thoughts, emotions, body, and speech. It's exhausting. I'm trying to improve. Maybe one day, it'll be an unconscious thought to use my body and mind as I used to without thinking about it. I'm not there yet, but that is my goal and I think I can reach this goal someday with help.

I was very thankful that Livia had a car, she could work babysit and visit me. For the next few months, she would go to work cleaning, then later either text me or talk to me on the phone until late. Or when I was lucky enough, she would come to my house to spend time with me until late. It kind of sucked for her to come to see me because she lived in Fort Myers; about 25 or 30 minutes away, depending on traffic those days when I could see her meant the world to me. I was freaking hooked. Many people say it was love at first sight, but I knew the first time I saw her in person that I would marry her. In fact, the first day I met her in person, I told her that if she needed to marry someone to stay in the country, I'd be all in. I said it as a joke. She came into the country with a six-month visa, but as we became closer and started to like each other more and more, she decided to take the step to extend her visa. It was for six more months.

Livia met a very nice and helpful lady who worked at a place called "Made in Brazil" as a paralegal. She was working on her schooling to become a lawyer. It was great that Livia met her at the Brazilian church before we met because this lady helped with everything involving visas for staying in America from Brazil. As I realized this was the girl of my dreams, I knew I had to keep her here in America as long as possible. She was the first girl I had met in Florida who was not scared of my disability. She became my best friend and quickly my girlfriend. It is a dream of mine to find a girl to become my best friend and lover. I've had other girlfriends, but none became my best friend. This was new and exciting, especially after my life changed completely. To me, it felt like she had been planted for me. I often lost hope throughout these very long and difficult 5.5 years fighting through this new life I had created for myself. My worst mistake was losing hope, not knowing what the future would have for me. As I was getting home from Golden, struggling each day emotionally and physically, and with all the many parts of my trustworthy brain I could no longer trust.

It was and still is the most challenging part of this process: realizing that I must be completely aware and conscious of every single step, motion, thought, and word that comes out of my mouth. When I could do it before without ever thinking about it, as I'm writing this right now it has been six years since the accident. I'm still learning daily about myself and how to control my body, especially my thoughts and emotions. I realized then that this would be my challenge until the end of my life, which I'm OK with. Like I told you before, my whole life, I've always prevailed through challenges I've faced. This will be no exception. It was cool for Mitch, my mom, and me that I had my girl-friend, Livia at this point, who would be there to help me through my recovery. It had gotten old enough to be taken to therapy so often and to look out for me when I fell, which was almost once or twice a day for years. This would be an immense weight off my parents' shoulders and my parents were very excited that I found someone who liked the new me. At this point, Livia's friends with the baby were moving to a house to with a room for her, compared to a mattress on the floor in the living room. I was sleeping on a mattress on the floor just like her, but I had my room. She was very excited to have a room. She went on Facebook Marketplace and found a nice bed. I helped her get her bed and things for her new room. We would switch between sleeping in her room and my room. It was incredible for me. I always dreamed that I would find a girl that my mom loved as much as me. She was the one.

22

Dream Come
True

Speaking of love, I was very nervous to tell her I loved her for the first time. I immediately loved her, but I had never said that to a girl. I wanted to make sure I meant it, which I did. It was just a big deal. I knew I felt it and wanted to choose the right moment to say it. I finally said it, and I'm glad I did because she reciprocated it. I knew that she was going to be my wife someday. Sooner than later. I decided to ask the question I had held since I first saw this Brazilian beauty. I wanted to propose to this girl. I knew I would marry her if given the chance and the opportunity presented itself. I was going to take full advantage of it. I planned to get her to drive us to our first-ever date spot, Manatee Park/Sirena Vista. I tried to keep it under wraps, but she had to drive me. I told her I had a surprise; I couldn't tell her where we were going. I plugged in the address on my phone map. I think once she realized where we were, she had the foresight to understand why we were there.

A few days or a week before this day, my parents took me to a nearby pawn shop to choose the perfect ring for my queen. It was a very nice sunny day; no clouds were in the sky. We sat on a bench looking at the water; at this point she knew what the intention was for this date. I was still working on controlling my body, which was the most damaged and affected part of my brain from the injury and, as far as I understood, was controlled a lot by the brainstem and other parts of the brain that controlled my extremities. I didn't trust my legs and body to be able to go on one knee to propose. I did it standing. I told her I would get better and be the man you deserve. I asked her, "Livia, will you be my wife?" She said yes, and we were engaged! Something I always dreamed of was happening, and all I had to do was fall off a cliff. Had I known that before, I would have done it earlier.

To be honest, I'm not sure if I was ready until then.

I had to learn much through this process, which made me a better man. This is the kind of man that Livia would want to marry. I have become less selfish since my life flipped. I cared too much about myself and not others, and I thought the world revolved around me to some extent. This must be something from John's genetics. My mother is not like that at all. I always tell people that this accident was the best thing that ever happened to me. It's most captivating that this happened to me (for more reasons than one) when I needed it so badly. It almost makes me feel like this whole falling was somehow planned, but who am I to say? I know that there are a lot of others who experienced terrible, heinous traumas, both more and less extreme, and they were not so lucky. I wanted to write this book to show that, with the right attitude and will, the worst trauma can be fought through in most cases, even with the most crucial aspect I was yet to recognize. Even in less severe cases there is always a way through. No, it won't be easy, but the struggle is the most gratifying part. In my circumstance it will always be a lifelong battle that I intend to win. No matter what the voice in my mind says, I will overcome. Even to this day, I still clash with my mind and the bad considerations that pop in, but I have learned to let them leave and go on with my day. Through long years of practice, I realized that hanging on to these notions did nothing for me. In the words of Dani Knight, it's OK to have these feelings and thoughts, but you can't be stuck in them.

Where was I now? My future wife Livia was gorgeous and very intelligent. Before she moved to the States, she was a civil engineer. A far cry from cleaning rental properties, but she knew she had to start somewhere. Once we were engaged, not too much changed. At this point in the journey, I realized that I had trouble controlling my emotions almost daily. The smallest things sometimes made me lose control of my emotions, usually anger or frustration.

In some moments, I would get so aggravated at myself that I would punch myself in the head. This happened more than I would like to admit. Once we got engaged, Mitch said it would be better to save money. She should move into our house and live in my room with me. I was very excited about it, and I guess it was good that she learned about how I am mentally and physically with my injury. It was a good thing for both of us. We packed everything from the house she lived including a bed. My first bed since I moved to Florida. The engagement and moving together were fun and exciting, especially because my whole family loved her. Gosh, my mom was beside herself with excitement to have another girl in the house for the first time. My mom has always been one of my best friends and supporters. The least I could do is marry a girl she loves and enjoys spending time with. All my friends were so happy I found a girl to spend my life with, even after my severe brain injury. Flutie knew how much I always wanted to find my soulmate. I guess I never found her because she was hiding in a different country. She continued working, and once we got engaged, everything changed for the better for me and her.

Livia was committed to making me better in every way she could. From devising exercises to do at home, getting us memberships to the gym, and, most importantly getting me back to therapy again. The virus was not entirely over yet. Still, she was prepared for when the therapy offices were opened again. In the meantime, she was always thinking about ways to push me physically and mentally, even until today. It was getting close to Christmas—the first Christmas with my family and my fiancée. By this point, I think Devin, my oldest little brother was preparing to join the Marines. So, my whole family got to meet her, which was awesome. My other little brother Shane was working, saving for college soon, and helping our family finances. Now that we were engaged, I thought that because her visa would run out in March, we should marry without much of a ceremony or her family being there. It was not ideal for her, but we decided that her whole family could meet me one day when I went to Brazil. Honestly, I'm slightly nervous about it because of my challenges. I will cross that bridge when I get there. We had a great Christmas, and the family met Livia, which was very important to me. As Mitch always says, family is most important.

It is so crazy to think back to all the awful times when I was depressed and thinking, "Man, I'll never find a girl to take all this on. I'll never find a girlfriend, not to mention a wife, that can deal with all my daily emotional changes and lack of control over both my brain and body." I think this experience showed me that there's someone for everyone. You must find the hope not to give up. Don't get me wrong; I lost hope for a long time, but I found it again, which is the important part. I'm not the only one who had to go through trauma before finding their soulmate, but they are there. As far as you know, they could be just waiting for you to become the person you must become for them to find you. I always keep this in mind: Mitch and my mom got married when Mitch was 32, and my mom had two kids already. Still, after becoming pregnant they decided to get married, and they have had a great marriage, raising four great men and living happily regardless of the many challenges they have faced. I think Mitch never thought he would marry a girl with two kids already, but sometimes that's how the world works. You don't expect to be where you are, but you do the best with what you have. I mean, I didn't imagine that Livia would move to America with the idea of marrying a man with a brain injury, but she fell in love. A dream come true for me since before the accident. I'm not sure if it was because she is from Brazil or what. Every single girl I talked to after the accident on Tinder was not about meeting a guy that could not drive, not to mention all the other problems that come with a TBI. Thank God she showed up on my app. Again, this was a plan in the making. Too many things that happened correctly caused us to meet like my parents searching for a place to move in South Carolina but ultimately deciding on Cape Coral, FL.

This would be the best decision my family ever made for me and the whole family. My mom especially found her dream job as a volunteer at a wild animal sanctuary. It was awesome to work with all these wild animals with some perks with it. We weren't far from the beach, like a 30–40-minute drive, depending on the traffic and the time of year. There were multiple different beaches we could visit around the same time frame. The thing we all missed the most was our friends from Maryland and family, but it was better we made this change. It was great that I could finally be in hot weather. From Maryland until I moved to Florida, I was eternally cold. It was not until I started doing the Wim Hof breathing exercises and taking a cold shower every day that my body temperature gauge, if that is such a thing, finally reset. It's also called the hypothalamus, which regulates appetite and body temperature. I no longer felt as cold after taking these cold showers for around one or two years.

It was only after I started going to therapy again that I realized that the cold showers and never getting hot were disrupting the nerves of my extremities, so I changed to taking a very hot shower and ending it with cold. I learned about this method once Brady shared it with me when I lived in Florida. Still, it made a huge difference. Another massive difference in my recovery was finally going to the gym again with Livia and strengthening my little legs. They needed a lot of work. I had lots of weakness in both legs, but my left has been much weaker since the accident. If you remember, I was partially paralyzed when I came out of my coma on my left side. The whole left side of my body is weaker than my right. Like the entire body. Everything from my arms and legs to my abs, even my tongue. To make things even more complicated, it was not just the strength that was affected but also the connection from my brain to my left side, making working out and using my body challenging. Things have gotten better over time. As far as I know, time is the best medicine for this injury.

Cannabis has helped me through the most challenging times of this struggle. It all started with having cannabis in my blood to stop the glutamate from releasing in my brain which was the first thing that could have saved my life before the doctors even had a chance to delve in. Through my research, I learned that those who have cannabis in their system during a TBI are 30% less likely to die during a TBI. It prevents the release of glutamate, a chemical in the brain that prepares the brain for death, and cannabis prevents it from releasing.

I smoked the most I ever had in my life the day before the accident. After the accident, after around a year and a half or two years, the emotional trauma was helped by cannabis. I was using far too much. I'm sure others have different experiences in their recovery process, but that was a factor that kept me from feeling like I had to end my life. I had such a great support system and a family that I love so dearly. I could not do that to them. Cannabis helped to take my mind elsewhere so I could leave those feelings and thoughts for a while. There were at least two or three years where this thought of death as an escape from the torment inside my mind was lingering.

To stop the physical and emotional anguish I experienced throughout. It plagued me. As you may recall, one of the first neurologists I saw after coming home from Golden plainly explained to me that if I needed to leave my mind for a time and do something to make me feel better,

I should smoke or ingest cannabis, but never drink alcohol. Alcohol does much worse things to the brain, especially a TBI brain. I quickly took this to heart. I'm not sure that's an excellent idea for everyone. I'm not a doctor. I didn't try until my brother invited me to join him and his friends. Who knows? It could have also been great for me before then or the opposite. I have no idea, but it helped me a lot when the time came for me to try. All I know is that when I finally started smoking after I got home from Golden, I thought about death daily. Maybe even killing myself, and I would have to fight these urges every hour. I know I could never end it on my own. I had that mental fight, with one side saying you could do it. Just end it. The part of my mind that wouldn't let me do it was almost an angel on one shoulder and a devil on the other. That was always raging inside at most moments. Cannabis was a better way to rest from the fighting than alcohol. And I'm sure if it was good or bad ever after the accident.

I'm sure that most people who have experienced trauma have/had these same feelings and thoughts. I realized this thanks to my little brother inviting me to smoke with him and his friends in his room with Rocco. It was the first time since this accident that I can remember having peace for about four hours. It was the greatest four hours I can remember since this whole mess started. It was for this reason that I continued to smoke every single day for the next few years. It kept me sane. When I thought I couldn't go on, what was the point? I'll never get better, which came daily even after all these years. Cannabis helped me fight these detrimental notions for a while. I never really talked about this, even with my therapist. Maybe writing it out and exploring these thoughts will do me well. It was exhausting trying to win this fight while improving with every step and every motion to return to normal. Or at least as much as possible. I think that this could be something that most people who don't have the experience of a traumatic brain injury won't fully understand. I have never explained this fight inside of my mind to anyone at every moment. This is why it's difficult for me to understand new information and learn new things quickly. There were always forces at work in the back of my mind trying to distract me from the task at hand. I have overtaken them from the onset until now. I thought I needed cannabis to get past my crippling depression and sadness after the extreme trauma and to take my mind somewhere else so I could relax. The problem was that when I got past this depression stage, I continued because it came habit or addiction. Not physically, but mentally. I should've stopped much earlier in the process of deeply exploring my inner mind. I've come to realize that I didn't need it. Still, I liked it for too many years. It was a great alternative to alcohol especially post-TBI. I am certain now that I could have found different and much better ways to deal with the depression involved in losing everything I was familiar with and completely starting over again. I was not ready then.

Flutie always knew that my dream was to be a great husband and father, based on the things I learned from Mitch. He was a great dad to kids who weren't even his. These lessons I learned as a husband and father passed on from Mitch's dad to Mitch and thank God for that one swipe to end all swipes. On December 10, I proposed after Livia got home from work. Livia did some very complicated math that was over my head and decided our wedding day would be February 3. We prepared everything for that day including a celebration with my family, Livia's best friends, and her family at their house. Livia put together awesome lights and decorations to make it look like an actual wedding reception at our friend's house with our Brazilian friends. One of them, an expert baker, made an incredible, delicious cake for everyone to enjoy. There was a lot of work to be done. I felt great about it when it was finished, and so did she. The next step was to make an appointment at the courthouse, pretty standard. Nothing to it. The day we planned to marry, we got our hair done and wore our Florida marriage attire, and my parents were with us. We were ready; we arrived at the courthouse and talked to the person at the desk. It was clear what we were there for. The man behind the desk explained that to get married you must make an appointment three days in advance. In other words, you must wait three days between the day you make the appointment and the day you marry. It's kind of a smart rule. I guess when people get cold feet, Livia and I were all in, no second guesses, at least for me. I cannot speak for Livia, but I knew she was the one. That was what I knew about Livia and still do.

Even though it was a difficult process just to move and figure out how to put my elbows on the ground to do different simple poses, somehow, she married me knowing the energy and patience needed to place me in the right place. All the years and tears I fought through about never finding a wife. Somehow, she was revealed to me from a different country. I have no explanation for that one.

We had to wait three days before getting married because we went to the courthouse on Friday. The person who does the marriages was not working until Monday. We didn't want to wait until Monday. Mitch, being the Jewish mafia kind of guy that he is, gave the guy at the desk some money and he agreed that on Saturday, he would come to Fort Myers and be the notary so we could officially get married with a ceremony in the street. We were in the street with Brady, my mom, Shane, and Mitch. I'm trying to remember; I think Mitch was not there for some reason. He had something going on. I think my mom or Brady recorded the whole thing.

It wasn't the most standard wedding, but we are

perfect for each other as they say in the Netflix show 'Dark'. We really are. After the wedding, we went to a local seafood restaurant and celebrated. Like most aspects of my life, it didn't go super smoothly but it got done. That was the important thing. Later that night we had the reception at our friend's house. My whole family was there except for Devin, who was in the Marines which I am still very proud of and will be until the day I die. Later that night, we went to their house where we ate and celebrated the big day. Livia and I spent hours buying lights and setting them up to make it a lovely party place to take awesome pictures. The only problem was that it was cold that night and we had to wear short-sleeved clothes. It was much worse for her to wear a pretty dress. She pushed through it, as did I. I am not as affected by the cold anymore since I started taking cold showers. It was still cold, though. I'm sure it was interesting for my family to go to this party with all these Brazilian friends who did not speak much English yet, but they made the best of it. They made a great first impression. Next was off to our honeymoon. For our honeymoon my parents rented us a nice hotel room in Estero, Florida, with a spectacular beach view and beautiful sand right outside our door. We were on the first floor, so we opened the screened door, and we were about 50 feet from the beach. It was a fantastic honeymoon, with incredible sunsets. When we got home, Livia had a plan.

23

Life
Changing

OK, where were we? Oh yeah, I just married the girl of my dreams. A girl I could only dream of finding, even after all the difficulties brought on by the horrific accident. I can only envision that she was a gift. This gorgeous girl was a godsend, as I was soon to realize. Even though I lost my faith in God after the accident, Uncle Billy had tried from time to time to get me back, to no avail. Thankfully, when I met my wife, who has been a firm Christian her entire life, she was inspired by her mother, or "Mae," as it is called in Portuguese. She went to Bible college and is very knowledgeable about the Holy Bible. I lost all faith for many years and didn't pray anymore. The more I spoke with Livia about faith and my struggles within, she always pushed me to get back to God, or "Deus." I started praying with her every night but felt nothing. I just did it to please her, not caring. My relationship with God was complicated. If God loved me, why the heck would He let this happen to me more than five years ago? I walked away from my faith in God after the accident with no real intention of ever going back.

Livia had a plan to get me back to therapy so I could continue improving my brain and body. Around this time, hospitals and therapy places were about to reopen after being closed because of the virus. Even before the therapies opened again, Livia was on a mission to get me back to being restored as much as I could. We were going to the gym as much as possible, usually creating stress and aggravation for both of us. Especially when I could not figure out how to move my body the way I must for the specific exercises; working out was my thing before. The effort to move my body parts correctly can sometimes be more challenging than the workout itself. Still, I must push on if one day I want to use my body as I did before when life was not always so exhausting. It was so curious that the first thing

Livia challenged me to do was try to have a day without a nap. Since the accident, I have struggled hard with mental and physical fatigue every single day. I started at Golden with breakfast, then speech therapy if I could eat yet, and right back to sleep before or after physical therapy. When I first got home from Golden, I would wake up, eat breakfast, talk to my family a little, and, before noon nap again.

This was my schedule until Livia challenged me to try not nap after breakfast one day and I would try occasionally. I would always wake up with her and make her oatmeal breakfast with either coconut milk, almond milk, or her favorite, chocolate almond milk. Oatmeal with a banana, blueberries, strawberries, and whatever else we could put in to make it better. Usually, almond butter or peanut butter. It is the least I could do to support my wife, who works daily for our family. I hope to return the favor to her by getting better one day. That is what marriage is all about, and love, for that matter. To this day, I always wake up with her before she goes to work. Depending on how tired I was after doing my morning chores I would sometimes still nap, I still grapple with fatigue daily. It is nothing compared to the start. I am confident that most people who have experienced brain injuries have or had this same trouble. Whether it is fatigue, confusion with small tasks, or correctly controlling my emotions, not to mention trying to control my body or walking.

Early on, when I first met my first neurologist, he explained to me that chronic fatigue is something I would have to find a way to manage for the rest of my life. I learned that if I don't have coffee when I first wake up, my brain doesn't wake up like before. I will crash if I don't get my evening too coffee or some caffeine, whether it be coffee or a pre-workout, by 5 o'clock. It's hard to stay up late. I think working out helps a lot as well. On days I don't work out for whatever reason I am much more tired by 9:00 PM. It could be a considerable amount more. A neurologist told me that after a brain injury, it's very good to get into a schedule and like most things in my life before, I would sometimes take things too far. Before I met Livia, I would always stop eating food at 7:30 or 8 to prevent me from getting overweight again, which was much of a fear so I started working out initially, and sports. I would eat at the same time every day. Sometimes the same foods, and always stopped at 7:30 PM or 8. Once a week I would stop eating food after lunchtime. I was unhappy with my body after I got home from Golden. I started working out when I could, walking on the treadmill or outside, and once a week I stopped eating food after lunchtime. I'm sure it was very bad for my brain after a brain injury. The brain needs those calories, but I had in mind that I would not have this body anymore. This was when I moved to Florida and realized I would not have much to do. I decided to get into good shape again through diet and home workouts. By the time I met Livia, my wife I was too skinny. I have a funny story about that. Livia and I started going to this awesome little French restaurant owned by a French couple. This place was incredible, a little place called "My Sweet Art" in Cape Coral, FL. We would go there occasionally for dinner or lunch and talk to the owner. One day, she told Livia she thought I was sick because I was so skinny when she first met us. That surely helped inspire me to eat more little by little.

Like everything in my life. I always try to push it to the limit, certainly concerning my body. When I decided I was going to get skinny again I pushed it too far. It was OK because Livia was there to help. As I quickly started that process, it was fun. I always avoided sweets and chocolates unless it was a special occasion or dark chocolate. Speaking of dark chocolate, it's funny, but every time I eat it I sneeze. I can tell if something is not dark chocolate because I won't sneeze.

I learned that it's OK to enjoy sweets and stuff occasionally. Quickly, it became a special occasion almost every night. After dinner every night we would eat ice cream. That was our way to gain weight. I decided to push myself to the limit until it became too much. When I married my soul mate then we started working on me more. At the same time, Livia was working on starting the green card process. Our whole family depended on Mitch and his uncanny ability to get everything done at all costs. No matter the circumstances, this always came in handy as he continued to come through. She got a front-row seat during the green card process to see his skill and madness. I'm sure this created stress for all parties involved. For those who don't know, a giant binder of documents needs to be filled out perfectly, or it will be sent back. This created more work on Mitch's shoulders, but anyone who knows him knows he doesn't stop until it's done. With his help, Livia's hard work on persistence, and the hard work and determination of the made-in-Brazil office the process had started. It's funny, but I think I married the Brazilian female version of Mitch, and I couldn't be prouder.

As this process started, I received a concerning letter in the mail around the same time. This letter from the Social Security Administration explaining that I would lose my benefits soon. I had been on disability since the fall; by this time, it was the year 2021. Once every year or two, Mitch always had to pull together a very tasking and lengthy document explaining that I'm still disabled. I'm guessing that this letter came because I stopped therapies for the length of the virus or a little bit before. This was because I had run out of appointments that my insurance would cover that year. I had to take a break until the following year came. The problem was that the following year was 2020, which was not an easy year. Then 2021 came. I guess because I stopped my therapies for a year or so, I was no longer disabled, or at least that is what it felt like for me and my family. This was a very long and extensive process to make sure I was still disabled. To be honest, it makes sense why they would do this. Five years post-brain injury is a long time and who knows what can be done in that amount of time? Not to mention all the people who abuse this system. I fully understand the reasoning for this. Once the letter came, it gave us the option to appeal this decision. We did, thanks to Mitch's quick thinking and understanding. This was a very confusing and unexpected letter. The letter explained that we must make an appointment to see a doctor. A Social Security doctor to see what my prognosis was now after all this time. Then we received another letter. According to the doctor's prognosis, this letter said that I'm good enough to work now. We strongly disagreed as I was still struggling with my balance and extreme fatigue. Then was the fact that I would fall on average twice a day for no apparent reason. All things that he could have never learned from my 20-minute appointment. I mentioned all the difficulties that I had to him. The next step was to get a letter explaining his findings. We patiently waited for the next letter. On it, the doctor explained that I was capable of working. At the end of the letter, it explained that we could appeal if you disagree with the doctor's findings.

Again, we did. Next time, there was a phone call in which someone called me for an interview, explaining all my daily activities and difficulties, which I had already explained to the doctor. This was more in-depth; again, they decided I could still work. We appealed again. The last step of the appeal process was to get a representative to help fight the case with me, someone with the experience and know-how to fight on my behalf. We were given a number to call for a representative to help fight this decision, which we did. This was a not-for-profit lawyer or paralegal. I had multiple phone calls with her, talking through my case, and she knew from the start that I had a good case. She just needed some more information from former doctors of mine and some more documents from earlier in my injury. I was nervous about what this could do for Livia and me one day moving out of my parent's house. We would need this income, but much more important than that, if I lost my health insurance. My seizure medicine alone costs $400 a bottle without insurance. This is crucial for my well-being and maybe the rest of my life. This was the most important aspect of this situation for us, not to mention the financial part. My representative for this process was very good and luckily, she had a good relationship with the judge I had to speak with as the last appeal of this decision. The day of the hearing was still in the heart of the virus, so it was a phone hearing. I was nervous, but my rep was on the phone which comforted me. It was a three-way call. It started with the judge speaking with my rep as she explained the appeal. They spoke for maybe 10 minutes, telling the story and all the evidence that she had. Then, the judge spoke with me for about 5 minutes and said, "You will keep your disability and all your benefits." The most crucial evidence came from the doctor at my first rehab facility, Golden Living. He explained that I'd be disabled for the rest of my life. Thankfully, this process was over. Our minds were at ease about this.

Now, it was back to working on the green card process, and Livia was trying to get her Civil Engineering degree from Brazil translated into English to be used to get a job in her field. She was always searching for employment in her field of civil engineering to start her career in America. As time passed and the green card continued, we had the goal that when her green card was completed, we would find her a job in her field and move out eventually. We were trying to decide if we should move up north, near Uncle Billy so Livia could experience the seasons and the snow. Just waiting for the green card to come in the mail. My family, however, didn't want us to move so far away. We ultimately decided to find a job for Livia somewhere in Florida.

24

Moving up in the
World

After some time of searching, Livia found a job in her field in Central Florida, more specifically in Leesburg, which is about 3 1/2 hours north of my parents' house. She spoke with the company and was offered an interview for the job. We jumped on it. She was very nervous and excited at the same time, and I felt the same way. After the interview, a day or two went by, and she had confidence that she did well and connected with her eventual boss. She was offered the job! Next, we had to find a place to live close to her job in Leesburg, FL. It was very difficult for us to find a place, with many people moving to Florida at this time. We were stuck and lost in the search, almost having to live in a hotel for the first few weeks of her employment.

We went to the Leesburg area to search for places to live, whether an apartment complex or a rental house. Unfortunately, we got nowhere. Eventually, we found one place about 30 minutes away from her job, which was not ideal, but we had no time. We chose this apartment complex without seeing it and hoped for the best.

My parents helped us pack up everything and move from our room in their house to our first apartment as a married couple. We were very excited, especially because we had never seen the apartment before we moved. It turned out to be just a regular, average one-bedroom apartment on the second floor with a nice little porch surrounded by trees which prevented natural light from coming in, something we didn't love. I guess beggars can't be choosers. Upon moving in, we had no idea about the area. Wouldn't you know it? Less than 10 minutes away is a great rehab hospital. We moved right next to The Villages, a large retirement community, like a whole town. The town we were living in is called Wildwood, not part of The Villages but the closest town to it.

The initial interesting thing that happened at our

new home occurred one day during the first week after moving in. For some reason, Livia and I started talking about my childhood and stepmom to Livia. One thing led to another, and I broke down crying to Livia for the first time. It was a good thing, too because until this point, she thought I could not express emotions and was somewhat concerned about this. That quickly changed this day as you will realize as you read on.

I started attending this hospital's occupational therapy (OT) and speech therapy I wanted to get more physical PT there too, but I had no more appointments available with my insurance. I had to wait until next year. Up to this point, I was still smoking cannabis every day and I even got a medical card for legal purchases. It became a habit for me at this point maybe even an addiction. I could easily go without it, but I just didn't want to. I met a neighbor and his family. He is a retired marine with a brain injury and we quickly connected over something in common. He and his wife both used cannabis for medical benefits him for his chronic pain from his military combat injuries and her for her anxiety. We both enjoyed talking and smoking and learning about his deployment stories. Every day I would work on this book and some therapy stuff, then go to his apartment to smoke and talk. To be honest, I was only wasting time smoking, with no benefit to me anymore. I was not physically addicted but mentally, yes. There was one time when I smoked with them and then went to OT. I could barely function on the tasks during the session. This neighbor and I became friends, and he drove me to therapy almost daily, a very nice dude. One day, I got too high at his apartment and was lying on the bed when Livia got home from work. After her day at work, she wanted to talk and started discussing something serious. However, because I was still high, I just could not stop laughing. I tried my best to keep it down, to no avail. This became the first intense fight we ever had in our new home. It was so bad that when she left the room I thought to pray for the first time on my own accord since the accident. I prayed that I could get past this addiction and take away this habit I had created. I told myself that I was finished with this. I meant it. Less than a week or a few days later (I don't remember the exact time frame), we were Face Timing with Livia's mom, as was our nightly ritual.

She started explaining a synopsis of Job's story in the Bible because I asked if God punishes people for their sins. She likened it to the way a father doesn't punish his child when they hurt themselves by accident after the father warned them not to do it. The child did it anyway, and now they are hurt. Similarly, God doesn't punish or hurt us, but we face the consequences of our sins. I was unfamiliar with this book or story, and Livia was translating what her mom was saying.

It's a crazy story. If you don't know it, I challenge you to read it. I won't spoil it for you, but she explained it. Job was a good God-fearing man who loved God wholeheartedly. He went through so much pain and anguish, losing everything he had and everyone he loved, much worse than what I had to go through. For a reason unknown to him. He never once cursed God. He questioned a lot, asking why. Little did he know, he was being tested. God gave the devil full authority to do whatever he wanted to him without killing him to see if Job would still love and worship God and not curse Him. He never once cursed God. I won't give away the ending, but it's a compelling story. It hit me hard, so hard. After the accident, and before I even started the band, I had walked away from God for no real reason except curiosity. It was not until this point in my journey that I understood why all this could have happened to me.

Like it says in my favorite Bible verse, Jeremiah 29:11: "For I know the plans I have for you declares the Lord, plans to prosper you and not to harm you plans to give you hope and a future." NIV. The next few verses are powerful too.

I had so many friends living without God, living for the flesh and fornication with no noticeable adverse impacts. So, why not try living for the world and not with God? That was my thought process before the accident. Not to mention, as a Christian, all my sins are forgiven through Jesus anyway. However, not until six years post-TBI did I finally understand what it is to be a Christian and how lukewarm I was. Regardless of my lukewarmness, God still spared me. I didn't fully grasp my halfhearted faith until later in the story.

Livia's mom continued the synopsis, and it became clear to me all the many ways I cursed and left God before and after the accident. Instead of thanking Him for sparing my life, it wasn't until this exact moment, talking to my mother-in-law, being translated into a different language by my wife, that I realized I had yet to repent for my many sins and apologize to God for leaving Him, especially thanking Him for sparing my life for the first time. My life was going in the wrong direction before; I was heading down to hell. Once I composed myself after crying so profoundly again I immediately started praying for forgiveness and repentance. This was the first moment I felt something different inside. After praying sincerely, we started reading the book of Job every night before bed.

A few days, maybe a week later, it was a beautiful night with perfect weather, and we decided to eat dinner on the porch. Livia was Faceting with her mom while we ate. I had no idea what they were talking about in Portuguese. Suddenly, out of nowhere, I got the strongest vision or memory as I was eating. It was so profound that I found myself there again (at least in mind and spirit, back in the coma; I knew I was there). I was instantly transported somewhere else. I found myself in a bright white room, a radiant white, a kind of white I had never experienced before. I looked up and realized it was Jesus Christ speaking with me. He spoke to me with the most loving and beautiful voice, saying, "I'm sorry you're just not ready." I immediately broke down, fully sobbing for the next 20 minutes and later too, as I attempted to finish my dinner. Later, I prayed for thanks and for being patient with me these six years after the coma. In His infinite wisdom, maybe because I left my false idol of smoking weed, I was finally ready to see this memory. It could be because I finally got into the Bible or both.

He showed me this, even though I completely left Him and lived with a false idol (marijuana) clouding my mind and spirit for so many years and lost my faith. Still, he not for one second left me. I was told many times, by many people at many different times, that 'God wasn't done with you yet.' He has a plan for you.' I just shrugged it off. For many years I lost my faith especially, after the accident. I didn't know what was ahead of me. This was the first step.

25

The Grace and Mercy
of God

On the following Friday, Livia went to work, and I had OT in the early afternoon. She was going to pick me up after work. I was sitting and waiting in a large, nice chair in the hospital lobby just waiting for her to pick me up after my appointment. She called me and told me she had a nail in her tire and would be later than expected. She had gone to two different places to get the tire patched. Hearing this news, I wondered, "What should I do in the meantime?" Before I had time to finish this thought, a lovely lady, whom I didn't recognize started a conversation with me. Being very talkative, I continued to converse with her. She explained that she had seen me before at the therapy upstairs, the one I had just come from. She had a stroke, and she was curious as to why I was there. Her name is Cindy. I told her my story, a very abridged version. Upon hearing this, she immediately exclaimed that I must meet this client ambassador in this clinic, right next to where we were sitting in the hospital. From the outside, this clinic looks very futuristic. I thought it was a spa at first sight. I never thought to look inside, being the frugal man I am. Before we entered, she asked me what I thought it was. I said an expensive spa. I was right about the expensive part. For the rest, I was way off.

She proceeded to introduce me to this client ambassador named James. He continued to explain what this place was. It was a hyperbaric oxygen clinic for healthy aging and brain trauma. I said, "What? I have a little bit of brain trauma." I gave him a little rundown of my story about the accident. We continued our conversation. Somehow, we got on faith, and he told me how he found faith in Jesus after living his whole life and having two kids. As we talked about our faith journeys, we connected at a very deep level. He offered to buy lunch as we discussed our lives and the Aviv clinic. By the time Livia got there, we were still eating and talking. As he explained it to Livia, he arrived and gave the whole rundown to her. The only problem was that it was far beyond our budget to improve my brain and body with this clinic. As the conversation progressed, James explained to us that there was a program called the Aviv Cares program. This program was severely discounted for those who couldn't afford it otherwise. He explained that the board chose one person every month for this discounted price. He said he would try his best to talk to the upper management to see if they could put me on the list for the next available spot for the Aviv Cares application. He said there was no guarantee, but he would keep us posted. That night, we returned to my parents' house for the weekend. My little brother went to work Saturday morning and asked if I wanted to smoke with him after work. I thought maybe and prayed, asking, "God, should I smoke or not? Give me a sign." I took a quick nap for half an hour and woke up to my phone ringing. I answered, and it was James from the clinic telling me with an excited voice. "Cody, I talked to the clinic and the team, and you are in." I couldn't believe it. There were three of these clinics in the entire world at this time. In Israel, where it was founded, Dubai, and Central Florida. In The Villages. This was as clear a sign as could be. I did not smoke that day. I have not even considered it since. The following week, I had my first appointment to meet Dr. Mo, the head doctor of the clinic, in which I explained my situation and the plan.

A week or two later, I went to the clinic for day one of the three-day pre-assessment exams. Nothing crazy, testing different things, including some mental testing like attempting to draw a 3D box, which I couldn't do at all. Some computer tests, too. Then, a quick breathing test to check my lung strength, some blood tests checking almost everything, and an X-ray of my lungs. By far the most interesting exam was a spec scan of my brain. They decided not to do an MRI because of the metal in my skull. I will try to put these pictures online or in this book, including a picture of my reconnected skull. The doctors in California had their hands full, fixing it the best they could. They did a great job with what they were given. Upon receiving the results, I was very excited to explore the damaged parts of my brain and what they control. In fact, most of my brain was at least somewhat damaged. It all happened for a reason. To bring me back to God, turning from my sinful ways and living for the flesh. I'm so incredibly grateful for this accident. If it were not for this accident, I have no idea how I would have found my perfect wife and my faith again. It is so curious to me how this all came to pass. I do not doubt this was His plan, having been so lost my whole life with no direction.

After I finished my pre-assessments, the next week I went into the chamber every day for hyperbaric oxygen therapy. Each time I entered the chamber, they called it a dive because it looked like a submarine, and the chamber put you in a place that felt like you were 30 feet under the ocean with that amount of pressure. The whole time you're in the chamber, you play brain games created for your specific brain difficulties. I started in the chamber for 20 minutes to acclimate to the pressure. After these first 20 minutes, you put on an oxygen mask and breathe 100% oxygen for 20 minutes. After these 20 minutes, you play these games to stimulate specific parts of your brain that need improvement. After this, you have an oxygen break for 5 minute, in which you breathe normal air, around 20% oxygen. Then, we returned to the games and oxygen for 20 more minutes. This cycle repeats three times until the chamber depressurizes at the end of the last cycle and you are done until tomorrow. The sudden change of oxygen makes the brain think you are dying, causing you to go into the fight or flight brain practice, causing the brain to release stem cells. Crazy, I know. There was a lot of damage to my brain, with the most damage being in the part of the brain that controls the use of the extremities. I met many friends throughout the process. The part of my brain controlling emotions needed work, which I can so clearly realize now too.

After dive #1, I felt nothing different. After dive #2, I went home and napped, as I'm known to do. Before I fell asleep, I was lying in bed, and somehow, I could see all these very quick-moving, almost like electrical circuits I could see in my brain through my closed eyelids. It was so incredibly intense. This was the first time I knew something real was happening in my brain. From that day forward I experienced this same thing every time I closed my eyes, getting stronger as the program progressed, especially before bed or a nap. Even today, it is not nearly as intense. I did the same routine the following week, except now I had daily appointments. The program was 60 dives over three months, every day, Monday-Friday. Sometimes PT, OT, speech therapy, and even occasionally mental therapy. This did not include the appointments with different doctors and other activities to teach my brain how to use my body correctly again. It is a very comprehensive program geared toward healthy aging and sometimes brain injuries, strokes, and any brain damage at all.

My appointments started around 10:30, depending on my schedule for the day. Every day, I would wake up around 8:30 or 9, eat breakfast, and drink coffee, and from the time I woke up to the time I left, I would listen to the Bible and enjoy every second of it. I tried my best to focus on each word. By the time I finished the program, which was Monday-Friday for three months plus 20 more dives due to the severity of my brain damage, I had 80 dives instead of the usual 60. One of the parts of my brain that was heavily damaged and is slowly improving is my short-term and immediate memory. I eventually listened to the whole Bible once and I decided to start on it again this time beginning with the New Testament. James was fired throughout my time in the program, which upset me. I didn't ask many questions. It could have to do with the fact that he started a Bible study with some people he met there. The first book we studied was the Book of Revelation, especially because of the things happening in the world now. It seems like we are living in the book of Revelation right now at least the beginning of sorrows in Matthew 24.

As I read and listened to the New Testament again, it became abundantly clear why this situation could have happened to me. It reminds me of Jesus's parable in *Luke 15:4-7: "Suppose one of you has 100 sheep and loses one of them. Doesn't he leave the ninety-nine in the open country and go after the lost sheep until he finds it? And when he finds it, he joyfully puts it on his shoulders and calls his friends and neighbors together and says, 'rejoice with me I have found my lost sheep'. I tell you that in the same way there will be more rejoicing in heaven over one sinner who repents than over ninety-nine righteous persons who do not need to repent." NIV*

Until I read or listened to the whole Bible and was re-reading the New Testament. As I got to the Book of Revelation, I fully comprehended what God had done for me. The way I was living at this time in 2016 was slowly dragging me down to hell. The third time I read the Book of Revelation, not too long ago I came across this verse, Revelation 3:19: "Those whom love I rebuke and discipline. So be earnest and repent." NIV. It took me a long time, but I finally did. It took me three times to read and listen to this book of the Bible to see this verse. Every time I get into the

Bible, it teaches me more. I was disciplined and rebuked with some tough love from God the Father.

Regardless, I eventually finished the program. Once I finished the whole process, I was always incredibly fatigued daily and nightly. I would sleep on various couches in the clinic from the fatigue while waiting for Livia to pick me up. The people working at the clinic said that extreme fatigue meant it was working and gosh, was it working. The doctors all said the extreme fatigue means it's working. It was kind of sad, but during the program, Livia and I received gym memberships and since I was always so tired, we didn't go as much as we wanted. In fact, there were multiple days I would get home from the clinic and sleep until the next day. Or if not, I would have to nap after I got home for hours.

At one point during the program, I learned to run again too. Not with great form, but I was excited to do it again and get my heart rate up. We would get home after the treatment for a week or so and then go to the nearby park and run. After this week, the therapists and the neuropsychologist told me that I was doing too much. It was messing up my brain improvements. Plus, my left knee joint was not strong enough to continue running. I had to stop. I have complete confidence that one day, God willing I will run again correctly.

Upon completing the program, I was exhausted for the next three months, and I didn't have any energy to go to the gym for as long as I would have liked but it was much-needed rest. It's normal to be so tired after the program for three months. At the end I redid all the exams I did at the start. The most interesting one was the brain scan again. At first, there were a lot of parts of my brain that were blue or black, which indicates very minimal blood flow. With an IV of dye showing the amount of blood flowing with different colors through radiation, I could see the different colors in my brain. The colors show where the blood flows well or poorly. The worst colors to see are blue and black. Black areas have the worst flow or no blood flow. The blue cells are severely damaged, and the white, green, and red are good colors to see. I'll have to put photos of all the pre-assessment exam pictures, the post and the differences on my website, Facebook or Instagram. I had a lot of blue on both sides of my brain. I'll also show one picture that demonstrates the differences and where the colors were improved. Pretty amazing! The first thing Livia noticed was my wit. We were slowly realizing that my brain speed was improving. I am still feeling the improvements. I am incredibly grateful that I found this place.

I was a different case, and they did a great job with my case. I will recommend this clinic to others! Something that blew my mind was that I could only write a few words with my hand before I started, but by the time I finished I could write again. Not beautifully, but before I could only write my first name. During each of the first 20 minutes of the dive, I would work on my writing, and now I can write. I thought I had lost this forever. The program was not easy and tiring, but it was worth it! If nothing else, to help fix my extreme emotional instability I have to say that many months after the program was completed for me, I am less fatigued throughout the day. Which is huge for me. The best part is that if I continue my brain training, the doctors say it can progress for months or even further. I thought there was no way to improve my brain after this horrendous damage I had acquired. God put me in the right place at the right time.

One random day, after completing the AVIV program Livia and I had to go to a store for something. We had two options; we could have gone to Walmart, which was further. Or Walgreens which was just down the road. After some decisive thought, we landed on going to Walgreens. As we shopped, I was looking through the vitamins. I observed a nice older man looking to find the zinc. Being a helpful guy, I helped him with his search. Throughout, he noticed my limp. I gave him a concise rundown of my situation, and I noticed he also had a limp. He proceeded to tell me his story. As we conversed, he told me he played basketball in the ABA. For those unfamiliar, this was the NBA before the NBA. Thus, he limps from a hip replacement. At some point throughout the conversation, I asked him if he was a Christian, and he was. In fact, he was a Christian author. Eventually, Livia went to find me and found me speaking with this gentleman. The thing that he said that hit me the most to this day was, "The first thing Christ will say to you when you enter heaven is, 'Who'd you bring with you?'" It's a powerful consideration, knowing that the only thing you take to heaven is people.

From that moment onward, it's always been in my mind to consider this question. Jesus may say this to me as I first enter heaven, I and comprehend his point he was trying to make. As a Christian, I must spread the gospel to as many people as possible. At this moment, it became apparent what a duty there was regarding this book and my life journey. This author is named William Loyal Warren. Lastly, he gave us a copy of the book he wrote called 'Jesus Rapture is Coming Soon.'

The only problem with this new yearning I found myself wanting to unearth is that the way I lived before I was genuinely reborn; I was not living the Christian way at all. I was living against many of the teachings of Christ, loving the desires of the flesh too much. Many people may not consider the drastic change I encountered through God, His word, and being spoken to by Jesus Christ. Hopefully, readers will take this story to heart and see that all things are possible with God. From where I came to where I am now. God played a giant role. He was not finished yet. I'm sure the apostle Paul may have felt the same way and maybe worse. This story can be found in the Bible in the book of 'Acts' Chapter 9. Where we realize that no one is perfect except for one, God. We all have things in our past that we are not proud of. Sometimes, we even reap the consequences of these actions. I experienced firsthand God's extremely gracious but firm hand. I knew all well what I was doing through my many sins and fornication. Still, He saved me and let me start my life again until I was genuinely born again through the inspiration given to me by Livia her wise mother, and ultimately Christ Himself.

A month or so after meeting this Christian author at Walgreens, we decided to finally go back to the gym after many months of not going except for some weekends. We returned to the gym with a membership courtesy of my new insurance plan. Someone who worked there welcomed us and shared some interesting news. Apparently, a member would often see us working out and notice my difficulties. This older gentleman was inspired by our effort and drive. He kept his eye out every day he went to the gym, hoping to find a way to help us somehow. Again, when I finished the program, I was too tired to go back to the gym for around three months. This man named Pat was feeling discouraged about not seeing us anymore. Finally, when we went back to the gym for the first time, a man who worked at the gym, maybe the manager came up to us before our workout and explained that there was a member of the gym who wanted to pay for me to be trained by a trainer at this gym. An anonymous member wanted to pay for me to be trained out of kindness. He didn't know that Livia and I had been arguing almost daily at the gym, mostly out of frustration and my pride. This was a huge blessing for both of us, another example of God using people to touch our lives. God stepped in. He saw that we were struggling to work with my anger or frustration. Little did I know what kind of training and trainer this would be.

That following Sunday, I received a phone call from the trainer who would work with me. We were both mind-blown by this man's generosity, and we were very excited to start this journey together. The trainer's name is Jason. Upon first meeting him, Livia, and I realized he was the most knowledgeable trainer we had ever met and had much experience working with people with body and brain connection problems. I learned he went through PT school and finished but couldn't afford graduate school. With all my body-to-brain connection difficulties, Jason had the know-how to try and get back to normal as much as possible. I'm incredibly grateful to Pat for connecting us with Jason. I'm fully confident that I'll walk well again, God willing.

I hope that through reading this whole story, you will realize that through unspeakable and sometimes impossible situations in our lives, God is there for you. Even if you walk away from God, He is there with open arms waiting for you to return, repent and accept Jesus Christ into your heart. Most importantly, confess Him as your Lord and Savior with your mouth. Your life will be forever changed like mine has been since my transformation commenced. I always go back and remember this verse:

2 Peter 2:20-22: "If they have escaped the corruption of the world through knowing our Lord and Savior Jesus Christ, and are again entangled in it, and are overcome, they are worse off at the end than they were at the beginning. It had been better for them not to have known the way of righteousness, than, after they have known it and then, to turn their backs from the holy command that was passed on to them. Of them the proverbs are true, a dog is returns to his vomit; and a sow that is washed returns to her wallowing in the mud. NIV

I think a good explanation of repentance is to admit your sin and quit it, in no uncertain words, turning away with the understanding of how much it hurts God. He genuinely desires all people to go to heaven, and it hurts Him when we sin. If you love and fear Him, you want to and will change.

I often returned to my old ways; I was no different than anyone else. Until I fully repented and had my heart changed through the Holy Spirit when the time was right. I'm not perfect; there's only one that's perfect and that's God. Also, Christ but He is God as a man 100% man, 100% God. I'll never be perfect, but I will strive daily to be more like Jesus. Looking back, like I do now I see that this extremely difficult and painful situation was the catalyst for saving my soul and humbling me. I didn't do it as gracefully as I hoped but it was all God's plan. God's ways are higher than ours. I didn't see the big picture at all. Had I been wiser, maybe it would have been abundantly clear. It wasn't. Instead, I was very confused and angry with God for the situation that ensued. If God truly loved me, why would He let this happen to me? Only looking back now do I realize I was physically strong through all this but spiritually weak.

As you can see now, God loves us so much that, unbeknownst to me He gave me the opportunity to start my whole life again. As Flutie put it, it was like watching a baby go from a newborn to four years old in 8 months. Only when I met my lovely wife and moved to our first apartment did I understand what He did for me. I'm certain that had this horrific accident not happened I would have returned to my old ways again. It's somewhat insane that even from early in the Old Testament when I was listening to the Bible as I did the dishes;

I noticed *Judges 10:10-13, "And the children of Israel cried to the Lord saying, we have sinned against You, because we have both forsaken our God and served Baals! So, the Lord said to the children of Israel. Did I not deliver you from the Egyptians from the Amorites and the people of Ammon and from the Philistines? Also, and Sidonians and Amalekites and Maonites oppressed you; you cried out to Me, and I delivered you from their hand. Yet you have forsaken me and served other gods. Therefore, I will deliver you no more." ESV.* God still delivers His people, with Israel being thier own country today.

God gives us so many chances to do what is right but our sinful nature, pride, and the desires of the flesh fight against our spirit. The graciousness and patience of God are unmatched. He loves us so much that even after we disobey time after time, sometimes intentionally; He doesn't leave us. In my case God gave me many different chances to live the right way, but I was so consumed with my selfish desires that He had to do something very remarkable for me to finally heed the warning.

Looking even further back in the Old Testament to when Adam and Eve ate from the tree, as my mother-in-law explained so elegantly, with Livia translating:

"But of the tree of the knowledge of good and evil you shall not eat, for in the day that you eat of it you shall surely die."

Genesis 2:17 ESV"And the woman said to the serpent, "We may eat of the fruit of the trees in the garden, but God said, 'You shall not eat of the fruit of the tree that is in the midst of the garden, neither shall you touch it, lest you die."

Genesis 3:2-3 ESV"And the Lord God made for Adam and for his wife garments of skins and clothed them."

Genesis 3:21 ESV"For the wages of sin is death, but the

free gift of God is eternal life in Christ Jesus our Lord."
Romans 6:23 ESV

God told Adam and Eve that if they ate from the tree of knowledge, they would die but when they did eat, they didn't die immediately. They died spiritually. That action created the separation between man and God. As it is stated in Romans, "for the wages of sin is death." So, death must happen when we sin. God accepted an exchange. A pure, innocent animal took the place of the man. The sacrifices of animals was a law of God. It is like gravity. If you jump from the top of a building, you will fall because it is a law. It must happen. In the same way, when we sin we must die. God, in His infinite mercy accepted the sacrifice of a lamb in our place. Jesus is the Lamb of God.

When Adam and Eve sinned against God, He killed the first animal to make clothes for them to cover their shame and sin. God performed the first sacrifice to save us.

"For we know that the whole creation has been groaning together in the pains of childbirth until now."
Romans 8:22 ESV

When man sinned, he cursed the earth. It is cruel and sad, but because of sin innocent animals had to suffer and die in place of man. That's why for each sin they had to sacrifice an animal. If a man died, he would go to hell with no chance to repent.

"And to Adam, He said, "Because you have listened to the voice of your wife and have eaten of the tree of which I commanded you. 'You shall not eat of it,' cursed is the ground because of you; in pain you shall eat of it all the days of your life."
Genesis 3:17 ESV God, in his infinite mercy, planned one more time to send the Lamb Jesus to die for all of us.

"The next day he saw Jesus coming toward him, and said, "Behold, the Lamb of God, who takes away the sin of the world!"

John 1:29 ESV

There's your little Bible lesson for today.

I hope this story and testimony can guide you and can be applied to your everyday life. Not only to improve your life but also those around you. I pray that everyone who reads this story will share it and use the lessons inside to strengthen your life and trust in God, knowing that all things are possible with Christ. No matter your situation, He loves you and will never leave you.

True story! I can't tell you how to live your life, but I can tell you that there's only one way to heaven—through Jesus Christ and continual repentance of your sins, declaring with your mouth that Jesus Christ is your Lord and Savior, ultimately being changed by Him.

Until these days, I never fully grasped the idea of the fear of God, as it explains in the book of Proverbs 1:7: "The fear of God is the beginning of knowledge." ESV. Now, after losing everything I had and worked so hard for throughout my life, it became apparent the authority that God has over our lives. If we stray from His plan for us. He can humble us. Through grace and mercy, He can give us many chances. It's up to us what we do with them knowing that it's Him that can sentence us. As a wise man once told me at Walgreens, Jesus will likely ask me who I brought with me when I go to heaven. Hopefully, spreading this story will help bring others with me.

It's curious; when I first got the idea to write this book, I was living in Maryland, and I had no intention of it concerning God. As you can see, I had no choice in the matter. From living with John, then my mom and Mitch, exploring faith with my high school friends and Uncle Billy/Aunt Kim, and all my misadventures before the accident and after. God never left me. He never does. It's astounding and irrational to me that God died for our wrongdoings against Him through Jesus Christ, who was God in the flesh, wanting to save us from our sins. Hoping that we would accept Him as our Lord and Savior. It costs us nothing, but it costed Him everything. That is the ineffable love He has for us.

I'll leave you with this, my favorite Bible verses. I guess I had to live it to understand and believe it.

Jeremiah 29:11-13 "For I know the plans I have for you," declares the Lord, plans for welfare and not for evil, plans to give you a future and a hope. Then you will call upon me and come and pray to me, and I will hear you. You will seek me and find me, when you seek me with all your heart. I will be found by you, declares the lord, and I will restore your fortunes and gather you from all the nations and all the places I have driven you, declares the Lord, and I will bring you back to the place from which I sent to you into exile." ESV

... To be continued...

26

In Memory of Anthony

Frasca

This was a very unexpected moment in the writing process of this book. It was a Friday night and I started working on this part Tony sent me maybe one year before. That day, I felt compelled to work on it. That same Friday, I texted him, but he never responded. On Saturday morning, I received a text from my mom showing in the newspaper that Tony had passed away. It ripped my heart out. I was crushed, and my family was too. I am incredibly grateful for the many amazing times we got to share. He was one of my best friends and will always live in my heart.

In loving memory of Anthony Frasca! A great friend, always there for me, especially during the hardest times. I love you and will never forget you. AYYYYA TONY!"

A letter from Tony
"When I first met Cody, we were in the same Honors British Literature class at North Carroll High School (Junior Year / 11th Grade). I knew Cody as a very popular, outgoing, and overall great guy. We bonded right off the bat and instantly shared a similar sense of humor.

In contrast, I was a pretty shy 16-year-old student who was anti-social with anyone outside of my core group of friends. I didn't play sports; didn't know many people in the grades below us; and was unsure of which clique I fit into.

From the day we met, I could tell Cody didn't see me the way I saw myself - he saw and treated me as a genuine friend of his. He introduced me to his other friends, and it finally felt like I was being accepted into an otherwise intimidating group of cohorts. It felt like I didn't belong at first, but everyone was just as kind and welcoming to me as Cody was.

Our relationship continued to grow as we started going to the gym together and hanging out more. He invited me to his house multiple times, where I met his wonderful and loving family, who accepted me just as easily as Cody did. I was extremely insecure, critical, and judgmental of myself, and was surprised how easy it was for these wonderful and kind people it was a breath of fresh air, and this gave me a level of confidence that I had never had before.

My family didn't do these things. Growing up in a divorced household and growing up impoverished, this type of family love was foreign to me. I would come over and it felt like everyone was so excited for me to be there and say (in an Italian accent), "AYYYYA TONY!" This meant the world to me in so many ways. Since then, I have loved his family and I always know I can come to them if I am ever in need.

After our senior year, everything about college was up in the air for Cody and me alike. Should I join the military? Should I take on this massive amount of debt? Am I even going to college? This was an inflexion point in my life, just as it was for Cody. Cody had the incredible opportunity to take his first year of college in Hawaii. He would post pictures on social media, and it seemed like he was having an absolute blast out there – as he should!

For me, I decided to enter the workforce via a wealth management firm and start a career in business/insurance/technology. It was good money, and I did this for about a year until I discovered the owner of the company, I was working for was a fraud. I left and enrolled into Carroll Community College (Carroll) to begin my 8-year journey through higher education and academia.

After Cody's first semester in Hawaii, money seemed tight as it was for everyone in 2008–2010 and he opted to come back to Maryland for school. Ultimately, Cody ended up where I was in my education journey, and we immediately synced back up as he was also enrolling into Carroll.

We immediately picked up from where our relationship had left off, as if he never left Maryland at all. We immediately resumed our friendly tradition and were back in the gym together and grabbing sushi from China Manor afterwards. He always taught me about how to lift and eat better. I learned so many nuggets of wisdom from Cody, and I'll never forget how influential Cody was in shaping a foundation for my health, life, and future.

When we would go out to parties together, we were bilateral wingmen. He would talk me up and introduce me to a lot of girls who were quite attractive. I never thought I would be able to even speak with some of these women, but they probably saw me with Cody and thought, "Wow, he must be cool if he's hanging out with Cody!" Whether this was true or not remains a mystery, but being so insecure at the time, this is exactly what I thought.

After we graduated from Carroll, life began to change drastically for both of us. We were faced with very difficult decisions on how to navigate our next steps through life and the unknowns of our career paths. The idea of needing to know everything about our future was daunting to say the least. We were lost together and trying to figure it all out, but we had each other, so at least we were able to laugh and have a lot of good times and memories along the way.

I was heavily invested in my business/technology career path, so I (kinda) knew what direction I wanted to go into. Meanwhile, Cody was lost in the fog. When we would hang out, he desperately asked me for guidance, and all I could do was try to simplify my approach: "just start doing something and you'll figure out what you do and don't want to do along the way." Easy for me to say as someone who was about to purchase their first house at the age of 23.

This made Cody and I closer than ever because I wanted to be there as a friend. He had been my friend in my darkest times, including my father's suicide, and I was committed to be there for him no matter what even, if it was just to watch South Park or grab some sushi.

Though he was lost, Cody remained focused and tenacious to find his way towards his future. He started playing and learning the guitar, and ultimately formed a pretty rad local band. Cody was an incredible singer as well, so if he was in front of a girl and played "Wonderwall," there was an absolute guarantee that said girl was probably going to kiss Cody that night he still had his looks and the moves, just like always.

At this time, I had started a relationship with a girl who would become my wife, and Cody was still trying to discover who he was and what he wanted. The dating realm left him heartbroken many times, and I would tell him, "Don't focus on women man just keep doing you for now," but of course, he wouldn't listen.

It was almost summer one year and Cody came down to my house just as he was planning to make his journey across the country to live and grow with his awesome brother Brady. Brady was a pretty radical free spirit who wanted to live life on his own terms, and Cody was in the same place.

I made us Chicken Chesapeake and I remember he took my shaker of Cheyanne pepper and wrote on the label because it wasn't spelled as it was pronounced (his words). Life was really good at this point, and I was on top of the world doing my thing. It wasn't always this way, and I still had many challenges ahead of me, but while Cody was over, none of that mattered. This was the last time I would see Cody for quite some time, so we spent a good bit of time bonding that day before he flew out.

Fast forward to the next month and Cody had been in California for a few weeks and seemed to be having a great time exploring and finding out who he was. I couldn't have been happier for one of my best friends, and it made me smile whenever I would speak with him on the phone to hear about what was going on out there.

One night, around 2am, I was oddly awakened by a text message from my friend Sean who said, "Have you heard from Cody's parents?" Confused, I responded, "No, what's up?" Sean then continued to inform me that there was an accident and sent me the article of a man who had fallen off the edge of a beach-side cliff and was flown to the hospital under critical condition it was Cody.

I immediately called his mother Bridget and she was in hysterics, as any mother would be when they learn on of their children had been involved in such a traumatic incident. She was beside herself and I was just as worried, concerned, upset... and overall heartbroken. No one knew what was happening, and we were all scared to lose one of the most wonderful people on this planet.

His family had flown out to California to be with him, as he was in a coma for at least a month. Once I learned he had awoken from his comatose state, I was washed over with relief that my friend was alive; however, the doctors said he will be permanently disabled for the rest of his life.

This emotional rollercoaster took its toll on all of us, but in time, Cody's mother, family, and friends coordinated a local golf tournament to raise money for Cody's extremely expensive medical bills. There were at least 100 people who showed up to this event to show support for Cody, and it was a great reunion with friends from high school.

When the tournament was over, we gathered in and outside the clubhouse to welcome Cody back home for the first time. It was incredible and I tried to be one of the first people to welcome him back.

Upon seeing him for the first time since he left for California, I struggled so hard to hold back tears, as Cody needed assistance walking around and greeting his friends and family. I vividly recall the first time Cody and I made eye contact. He stared blankly at me for what felt like 15 seconds, and I could tell he had no idea who I was. As I was about to help him remember my name, he yelled, "TONY TONY TONY!!!" and did his best to give me a hug. After our moment, he proceeded to greet everyone else who was there to see him, and I had left with my girlfriend Erica to go to our car. I immediately broke down in tears.

I explained to Erica how sad I was about the prompting

even that had led me to feel so sad, and she consoled me the whole way home. I was so happy to see Cody alive and be with my best friend once more, but the thought of him losing his memory and all the wonderful times we had together overwhelmed me with emotion. This was one of the toughest days of my life.

From there on, I would visit Cody in the rehab facility in Westminster to keep him company and lend support in any way I could. I gave him a laptop of mine so he could watch things or do whatever, but his left wrist was broken so we ended up laughing and talking about all the things he was going through instead. It was lonely in there for him, and I knew it. I wanted to be the friend he would have been to me if I were in the same situation, and I loved him too much to not be there as often as I could.

After meeting with him on multiple occasions, I could instantly tell Cody was frustrated. Cody had always been the person to never make excuses in life, and this was no exception. He was determined to get his life back on track and resume his livelihood as much as possible before the incident, but the doctors and nurses were not convinced he would resume any dialectical or motor skills to the degree he once had, or even a fraction of his previous capabilities at that.

None of this mattered to Cody, and for the next several weeks in rehab, Cody was determined to kick rehab's a**, and he did. While Cody still had a long road ahead, he did not give up or falter his focus. Rehab continued outside of the facility for Cody, including speech, writing, and all sorts of physical therapy. He was fiercely determined, and I knew the real Cody hadn't been lost at all, and that's all he needed to keep pushing forward.

Fast forward about a year later and Cody's family was in the process of permanently moving to Florida. I would speak with Cody about this every time we met to gauge how he felt about this big move, and, though he would prefer to stay in Maryland with his friends, he knew this was the best next step for he and his family.

At this point, Cody had made a remarkable, statistically improbably amount of progress with his speech, writing, and mobility. He proved all the doctors wrong and wasn't even close to finishing his journey to recover.

Once Cody and his family moved to Florida, I planned my trip to Florida. By coincidence, Erica's brother Harrison and his now-wife Brooke were living in Florida, about 2-hours from where Cody was. It was the perfect excuse for a vacation, and I couldn't wait to visit him.

When the trip finally came, I drove to his family's new house and Cody, and I went out to a downtown area for pizza and Red Bull. Cody was always tired, so coffee and Red Bull were a big deal for me and him at the time. We went to the beach and took some pictures together. He was shy about pictures and was unsure how he felt about me posting these on social media, so I honored not to post any more online but that didn't stop me from taking more pictures with my best friend.

Cody had a lot on his mind that he wanted to talk about, including girls. I was a little annoyed by this because I vehemently continued to remind him that he needs to focus on himself instead of constantly being rejected by women. Cody had the moves – no doubt – but when it came time to have a first date, that's when things would fall apart. He was in a vicious cycle, but also had interest in volunteer work while he was down in Florida.

Unfortunately, Cody's family was limited on resources, and committing to driving Cody around and overseeing him while he volunteered was not a probable reality. Again, Cody was frustrated and felt lost, and I knew.

After dropping him back off at his parent's house, I left feeling a mix of emotions. I would discover later in life that I have Severe Bi-Polar Disorder and did not know how to process or communicate my emotions properly, and I ended up ruining the rest of my vacation because of this. I was frustrated and stressed, both in my professional and personal life, but I did not know how to solve *this problem. Nevertheless, I still loved Cody and returned home with a hopeful heart.*

Months later, Cody would have the opportunity to take a flight to Maryland to change his residency from Maryland to Florida. I had always told him that he would have a place to stay at my house, and I welcomed him to stay with Erica and I before passing him off to his family that would soon take him to meet relatives in Philadelphia.

If I recall correctly, I remember picking Cody up from BWI and we caught up on the drive back to my place. We setup a slumber party-esque scene in the basement to watch south park and enjoy the snacks and food we had gotten from the grocery store. Of course, we also made a run to Starbucks to make sure he didn't fall asleep too early.

This was a challenging event for us, as Erica and I had no idea how to accommodate someone with a disability, but Cody did an excellent job at guiding us. I gave him my comfiest clothes to sleep in and he liked them so much that I let him keep them. He was so grateful for our hospitality, and I was more than happy to be here for him as much as I could. The next day, I would drop him off at a relative's house in Maryland, which would be a checkpoint along the way to see his family in Philly.

Over the next several months, Cody and I continued to facetime and text each other as much as possible. I didn't like Face-Time a lot, but I know he wanted to see my face and hear my voice, so I made an exception. He would talk about all the things he wanted to do public speaking, a blog, a podcast, writing a book, volunteering, and of course, meeting girls.

It was hard to keep up with contact over the years be-cause life became busy, and I was very career-driven at this point. Not knowing I had Bi-Polar disorder, I would get easily frustrated with everyone, including Cody. In hindsight, I acted like such an ass, but Cody continued to accept me for who I am.

In 2020, Cody and I chatted on the phone, and he in-

formed me that he had a new girlfriend, Livia! I had so many questions and was a little concerned, but he assured me that they loved each other, and she didn't judge or see him any differently just because he was disabled. It was apparent that this was a perfect match for two wonderful and loving people.

Fast-forward to 2021, they were happily engaged and entered an even more committed relationship with each other. I was so happy for them, even though my life was shattering. In 2020, I discovered I had a mental illness; lost my job; and was separated from my wife which ultimately led to our divorce. My life felt over at times, and depression hit me harder than any other episode in my life. Waking up and crying was a daily routine, but then my routine became calling Cody and speaking with him at least once a week.

Hearing his voice and seeing his face reminded me of the many wonderful things that I had been blessed with in my life. He was a beacon of hope for me, just as I imagine I was for him during his days of suffering. I honestly cannot recall what we would talk about, but I always left our conversations feeling more motivated and positive than before the call Cody was always there for me.

Life for Cody and me has been an emotional rollercoaster, and it's impossible to believe that we're already 30-years-old. While we both have had friends who drifted away since high school, somehow, we always came back to each other and exchanged laughs. I am thankful and lucky to have had Cody in my life and am proud of how far we both have come. While our paths lead us in different directions, we always knew we could count on each other to keep our heads up.

I am beyond happy for Cody and Livia and cannot wait to spend many more years sharing laughs and creating new memories together."

Acknowledgements

I first want to thank each one of you that decided to buy this book. I'm incredibly grateful that I can use my experiences to help and inspire others. As you can see now, if you have made it this far in the story. I could not have done it alone. Especially, with my lack of familiarity of any publishing understanding or know how. Needless to say, I required much help. First, I should thank my godmother, Melissa who would type my voice messages into a Word document at the start. Then my supportive wife who at the time was my first girlfriend since the accident, Livia who became my typist for this project. Then Brady and my parents to fill in some details I didn't know or remember.

Next, my awesome friend Barb who read the first draft and gave me notes. Similarly, my Aunt Karen who did the same. I can't forget Uncle Billy and Aunt Kim who guided me through the whole process, being published authors themselves. I am very appreciative I had the opportunity to work with such a great editor as Tiana J. on Fiverr. I'm certain without her expertise, this book would be much less enjoyable to read. Lastly, I would like to thank my awesome brother-in-law, Francisco Alves da Silva for creating and designing this book in such a beautiful way.

Most importantly I'd like to thank Jesus Christ, my Lord and savior for saving me when I didn't deserve it. Ultimately giving me the chance to tell this story. Providing new mercies every day. This book is for You.

5 STORIES
DOWN

Sometimes you must fall to rise
CODY RIDENOUR

Designed by:

Made in the USA
Columbia, SC
10 August 2024

40277427R00167